# Salvador Dali

## CONSULTING EDITORS

# Salvador Dali

*David Carter*

**CHELSEA HOUSE PUBLISHERS**

NEW YORK ■ PHILADELPHIA

**CHELSEA HOUSE PUBLISHERS**

Editorial Director: Richard Rennert
Executive Managing Editor: Karyn Gullen Browne
Copy Chief: Robin James
Picture Editor: Adrian G. Allen
Art Director: Robert Mitchell
Manufacturing Director: Gerald Levine

HISPANICS OF ACHIEVEMENT
Senior Editor: Philip Koslow

Staff for *SALVADOR DALÍ*
Editorial Assistants: Mary B. Sisson, Annie McDonnell
Designer: M. Cambraia Magalhães
Picture Researcher: Ellen Barrett Dudley

ON THE COVER: Detail from *The Ecumenical Council* (1960), by Salvador Dalí. The entire painting is reproduced on page 102.

First Printing
1   3   5   7   9   8   6   4   2

Library of Congress Cataloging-in-Publication Data
Carter, David
Salvador Dalí / David Carter.
p. cm.—(Hispanics of achievement)
Includes bibliographical references and index.
0-7910-1778-8
0-7910-3015-6 (pbk.)
1. Dalí, Salvador, 1904–1989—Juvenile literature. 2. Artists—Spainsh—Biography—
Juvenile literature. [1. Dalí, Salvador, 1904–1989. 2. Artists. 3. Painting, Spanish. 4.
Painting, Modern—20th century—Spain.] I. Title. II. Series.
N7113.D3C75 1994
759.6—dc20
94-9735
[B]
CIP
AC

# CONTENTS

Hispanics of Achievement                        7

"I Withdraw"                                    15

The Seeds of Ambition                          21

Madrid                                         35

The Shock of the New                           49

Scandalous Success                             61

The Paintings of Salvador Dalí                 65

Independence of the Imagination                83

Classical Nuclear Art                          97

"Avida Dollars"                               105

Chronology                                    112

Further Reading                               115

Index                                         117

JOAN BAEZ
*Mexican-American folksinger*

RUBÉN BLADES
*Panamanian lawyer and entertainer*

JORGE LUIS BORGES
*Argentine writer*

PABLO CASALS
*Spanish cellist and conductor*

MIGUEL DE CERVANTES
*Spanish writer*

CESAR CHAVEZ
*Mexican-American labor leader*

JULIO CÉSAR CHÁVEZ
*Mexican boxing champion*

EL CID
*Spanish military leader*

HENRY CISNEROS
*Mexican-American political leader*

ROBERTO CLEMENTE
*Puerto Rican baseball player*

SALVADOR DALÍ
*Spanish painter*

PLÁCIDO DOMINGO
*Spanish singer*

GLORIA ESTEFAN
*Cuban-American singer*

GABRIEL GARCÍA MÁRQUEZ
*Colombian writer*

FRANCISCO JOSÉ DE GOYA
*Spanish painter*

JULIO IGLESIAS
*Spanish singer*

RAUL JULIA
*Puerto Rican actor*

FRIDA KAHLO
*Mexican painter*

JOSÉ MARTÍ
*Cuban revolutionary and poet*

RITA MORENO
*Puerto Rican singer and actress*

PABLO NERUDA
*Chilean poet and diplomat*

OCTAVIO PAZ
*Mexican poet and critic*

PABLO PICASSO
*Spanish artist*

ANTHONY QUINN
*Mexican-American actor*

DIEGO RIVERA
*Mexican painter*

LINDA RONSTADT
*Mexican-American singer*

ANTONIO LÓPEZ DE SANTA ANNA
*Mexican general and politician*

GEORGE SANTAYANA
*Spanish philosopher and poet*

JUNÍPERO SERRA
*Spanish missionary and explorer*

LEE TREVINO
*Mexican-American golfer*

PANCHO VILLA
*Mexican revolutionary*

**CHELSEA HOUSE PUBLISHERS**

# HISPANICS OF ACHIEVEMENT

*Rodolfo Cardona*

The Spanish language and many other elements of Spanish culture are present in the United States today and have been since the country's earliest beginnings. Some of these elements have come directly from the Iberian Peninsula; others have come indirectly, by way of Mexico, the Caribbean basin, and the countries of Central and South America.

Spanish culture has influenced America in many subtle ways, and consequently many Americans remain relatively unaware of the extent of its impact. The vast majority of them recognize the influence of Spanish culture in America, but they often do not realize the great importance and long history of that influence. This is partly because Americans have tended to judge the Hispanic influence in the United States in statistical terms rather than to look closely at the ways in which individual Hispanics have profoundly affected American culture. For this reason, it is fitting that Americans obtain more than a passing acquaintance with the origins of these Spanish cultural elements and gain an understanding of how they have been woven into the fabric of American society.

It is well documented that Spanish seafarers were the first to explore and colonize many of the early territories of what is today called the United States of America. For this reason, stu-

dents of geography discover Hispanic names all over the map of
the United States. For instance, the Strait of Juan de Fuca was
named after the Spanish explorer who first navigated the waters
of the Pacific Northwest; the names of states such as Arizona (arid
zone), Montana (mountain), Florida (thus named because it was
reached on Easter Sunday, which in Spanish is called the feast of
Pascua Florida), and California (named after a fictitious land in
one of the first and probably the most popular among the Spanish
novels of chivalry, *Amadis of Gaul*) are all derived from Spanish;
and there are numerous mountains, rivers, canyons, towns, and
cities with Spanish names throughout the United States.

Not only explorers but many other illustrious figures in
Spanish history have helped define American culture. For example, the 13th-century king of Spain, Alfonso X, also known as
the Learned, may be unknown to the majority of Americans, but
his work on the codification of Spanish law has greatly influenced
the evolution of American law, particularly in the jurisdictions of
the Southwest. For this contribution a statue of him stands in the
rotunda of the Capitol in Washington, D.C. Likewise, the name
Diego Rivera may be unfamiliar to most Americans, but this
Mexican painter influenced many American artists whose paintings, commissioned during the Great Depression and the New
Deal era of the 1930s, adorn the walls of government buildings
throughout the United States. In recent years the contributions of
Puerto Ricans, Mexicans, Mexican Americans (Chicanos), and
Cubans in American cities such as Boston, Chicago, Los Angeles,
Miami, Minneapolis, New York, and San Antonio have been
enormous.

The importance of the Spanish language in this vast cultural
complex cannot be overstated. Spanish, after all, is second only to
English as the most widely spoken of Western languages within
the United States as well as in the entire world. The popularity of
the Spanish language in America has a long history.

In addition to Spanish exploration of the New World, the
great Spanish literary tradition served as a vehicle for bringing the

language and culture to America. Interest in Spanish literature in America began when English immigrants brought with them translations of Spanish masterpieces of the Golden Age. As early as 1683, private libraries in Philadelphia and Boston contained copies of the first picaresque novel, *Lazarillo de Tormes*, translations of Francisco de Quevedo's *Los Sueños*, and copies of the immortal epic of reality and illusion *Don Quixote*, by the great Spanish writer Miguel de Cervantes. It would not be surprising if Cotton Mather, the arch-Puritan, read *Don Quixote* in its original Spanish, if only to enrich his vocabulary in preparation for his writing *La fe del cristiano en 24 artículos de la Institución de Cristo, enviada a los españoles para que abran sus ojos* (The Christian's Faith in 24 Articles of the Institution of Christ, Sent to the Spaniards to Open Their Eyes), published in Boston in 1699.

Over the years, Spanish authors and their works have had a vast influence on American literature—from Washington Irving, John Steinbeck, and Ernest Hemingway in the novel to Henry Wadsworth Longfellow and Archibald MacLeish in poetry. Such important American writers as James Fenimore Cooper, Edgar Allan Poe, Walt Whitman, Mark Twain, and Herman Melville all owe a sizable debt to the Spanish literary tradition. Some writers, such as Willa Cather and Maxwell Anderson, who explored Spanish themes they came into contact with in the American Southwest and Mexico, were influenced less directly but no less profoundly.

Important contributions to a knowledge of Spanish culture in the United States were also made by many lesser known individuals—teachers, publishers, historians, entrepreneurs, and others—with a love for Spanish culture. One of the most significant of these contributions was made by Abiel Smith, a Harvard College graduate of the class of 1764, when he bequeathed stock worth $20,000 to Harvard for the support of a professor of French and Spanish. By 1819 this endowment had produced enough income to appoint a professor, and the philologist and humanist George Ticknor became the first holder of the Abiel

Smith Chair, which was the very first endowed Chair at Harvard University. Other illustrious holders of the Smith Chair would include the poets Henry Wadsworth Longfellow and James Russell Lowell.

A highly respected teacher and scholar, Ticknor was also a collector of Spanish books, and as such he made a very special contribution to America's knowledge of Spanish culture. He was instrumental in amassing for Harvard libraries one of the first and most impressive collections of Spanish books in the United States. He also had a valuable personal collection of Spanish books and manuscripts, which he bequeathed to the Boston Public Library.

With the creation of the Abiel Smith Chair, Spanish language and literature courses became part of the curriculum at Harvard, which also went on to become the first American university to offer graduate studies in Romance languages. Other colleges and universities throughout the United States gradually followed Harvard's example, and today Spanish language and culture may be studied at most American institutions of higher learning.

No discussion of the Spanish influence in the United States, however brief, would be complete without a mention of the Spanish influence on art. Important American artists such as John Singer Sargent, James A. M. Whistler, Thomas Eakins, and Mary Cassatt all explored Spanish subjects and experimented with Spanish techniques. Virtually every serious American artist living today has studied the work of the Spanish masters as well as the great 20th-century Spanish painters Salvador Dalí, Joan Miró, and Pablo Picasso.

The most pervasive Spanish influence in America, however, has probably been in music. Compositions such as Leonard Bernstein's *West Side Story*, the Latinization of William Shakespeare's *Romeo and Juliet* set in New York's Puerto Rican quarter, and Aaron Copland's *Salon Mexico* are two obvious examples. In general, one can hear the influence of Latin rhythms—from tango to mambo, from guaracha to salsa—in virtually every form of American music.

This series of biographies, which Chelsea House has published under the general title HISPANICS OF ACHIEVEMENT, constitutes further recognition of—and a renewed effort to bring forth to the consciousness of America's young people—the contributions that Hispanic people have made not only in the United States but throughout the civilized world. The men and women who are featured in this series have attained a high level of accomplishment in their respective fields of endeavor and have made a permanent mark on American society.

The title of this series must be understood in its broadest possible sense: The term *Hispanics* is intended to include Spaniards, Spanish Americans, and individuals from many countries whose language and culture have either direct or indirect Spanish origins. The names of many of the people included in this series will be immediately familiar; others will be less recognizable. All, however, have attained recognition within their own countries, and often their fame has transcended their borders.

The series HISPANICS OF ACHIEVEMENT thus addresses the attainments and struggles of Hispanic people in the United States and seeks to tell the stories of individuals whose personal and professional lives in some way reflect the larger Hispanic experience. These stories are exemplary of what human beings can accomplish, often against daunting odds and by extraordinary personal sacrifice, where there is conviction and determination. Fray Junípero Serra, the 18th-century Spanish Franciscan missionary, is one such individual. Although in very poor health, he devoted the last 15 years of his life to the foundation of missions throughout California—then a mostly unsettled expanse of land—in an effort to bring a better life to Native Americans through the cultivation of crafts and animal husbandry. An example from recent times, the Mexican-American labor leader Cesar Chavez battled bitter opposition and made untold personal sacrifices in his effort to help poor agricultural workers who have been exploited for decades on farms throughout the Southwest.

The talent with which each one of these men and women may have been endowed required dedication and hard work to develop and become fully realized. Many of them have enjoyed rewards for their efforts during their own lifetime, whereas others have died poor and unrecognized. For some it took a long time to achieve their goals, for others success came at an early age, and for still others the struggle continues. All of them, however, stand out as people whose lives have made a difference, whose achievements we need to recognize today and should continue to honor in the future.

# Salvador Dali

*Salvador Dalí attends an exhibition of his work at New York's Museum of Modern Art in 1936. After being expelled from art school as a teenager, Dalí launched one of the most spectacular careers in modern art.*

# "I WITHDRAW"

Summer was just beginning in June 1926 when a 22-year-old art student named Salvador Dalí appeared for his examination by a jury of art professors at Madrid's prestigious San Fernando Institute of Fine Arts. His entrance into the large, crowded room caused a noticeable stir. Dalí always dressed with studied elegance, sporting flowing ties and often wearing a sky-blue silk shirt with sapphire cufflinks to set off his expensive tweed suits. In addition, he soaked his long black hair with brilliantine and then carefully varnished it with real lacquer. His odd dress and appearance aside, the professors knew that Dalí's behavior had been rowdy enough at times to cause his suspension from the institute three years earlier.

Still, if Dalí's conduct had been outrageous at times, he had worked harder than almost any other student at the institute, and there was no doubt that he took his studies quite seriously. Dalí had not only attended his classes regularly; he was often so absorbed in his painting that he would lose track of time, going hungry because he showed up in the student dining hall only after the meal was over. Although he was clearly influenced by the most daring painters of the day, such as Giorgio de Chirico and Pablo Picasso, Dalí also showed his respect for tradition by carefully studying the works of great masters of classical painting, such as Leonardo da Vinci and Michelangelo Buonarroti. He had continually pressed his professors for answers about basic painting methods: What was

15

the best way to mix oil? What technique should he follow to obtain some particular effect?

There was also no denying Dalí's gift for painting. His canvases had often been praised both within and outside the school as showing great talent and a marked originality. When Dalí's work had first appeared at an exhibition in his hometown of Figueres along with the work of 29 other local artists, the art critic for the newspaper *Empordà Federal* had singled out his canvases, predicting that the 14-year-old student would be a great painter. Because of Dalí's unusual talent, the San Fernando Institute had broken its extremely rigid admission rules, accepting the young painter even though he had turned in his drawing for the entrance examination on paper that was the wrong size.

When Dalí came before the final jury in June 1926, he had already completed the long series of examinations that all graduating students had to pass. It was now the duty of this jury to examine Dalí on the theory of fine arts. If he answered their questions competently, he would have his degree. Everyone expected the young painter to clear the final hurdle easily—he had been writing about art theory since the age of 15 and had read voraciously on the subject.

The professors on the jury had every reason to believe that Dalí was eager to get his degree. They had heard rumors of his father's sometimes violent disposition and knew that the elder Dalí had insisted on his son's attending the institute. Skeptical about the possibility of anyone making a living by painting, Dalí's father had convinced Salvador to earn a degree in fine arts so that he would be qualified to teach art. That way, the senior Dalí reasoned, his son could at least be assured of a steady income as a professor and would not end up living in poverty as had Ramón Pitxot, a close family friend who was a struggling artist in Paris.

The procedure for the examination required the students to draw lots for the subject they had to speak about. Dalí's subject turned out to be the Italian Renaissance artist Raphael, one of his favorite painters. The jury fixed their gaze on Dalí, expecting to hear him expound brilliantly on an artist he admired so greatly and whose work he knew intimately. To their amazement, Dalí replied, "Gentlemen, with all due respect it is impossible for me to talk about this in front of these three professors because I know much more about Raphael than all of you put together."

Dalí's answer caused a tremendous uproar in the room, but Dalí simply walked out of the auditorium. He was immediately dismissed from the San Fernando Institute, the expulsion later made official by an order signed by the king of Spain himself, Alfonso XIII, and published in *La Gaceta,* a leading Madrid newspaper.

After walking out of the examination, Dalí returned to his rooms at the Residencia de Estudiantes (Students' Residence), where he had passed many memorable days and evenings with a group of friends, among them the future filmmaker Luis Buñuel and Federico García Lorca, who would become perhaps the greatest Spanish poet of the 20th century. In 1926, Buñuel and Lorca were simply close friends who had joined with Dalí and other students to form a kind of club. The students would meet in cafés or hotels, discussing literature, painting, and philosophy or simply drinking and carousing, depending on their mood. They made up sophisticated word games and indulged in various pranks, such as tying up traffic in the middle of Madrid by standing at busy intersections and staring upward, pretending to see something marvelous in the sky. They put on plays and spent hours listening to American jazz on their gramophones. In short, the high-spirited group pursued the kinds of serious and playful endeavors common to students of their age.

Now Dalí had to say good-bye to the friendships and memories the Residencia held for him. He did not do so lightly. Many of his actions were designed to shock people, but many also had a serious purpose behind them, including his decision to engineer his own expulsion. Dalí knew that he had outgrown the San Fernando Institute. He felt he had learned all that it could teach him. In fact, it was the professors' seeming lack of seriousness that had alienated Dalí. When he had asked a technical question in all sincer-

*Dalí began* Portrait of My Sister *in 1923, when he was 19. After meeting his fellow painter Pablo Picasso four years later, Dalí painted over the original to mirror Picasso's style: the face at the top is almost all that remains of the original work.*

ity, one professor had vaguely replied, "My friend, everyone must find his own manner; there are no laws in painting. Interpret—interpret everything. . . . It's temperament, temperament that counts." The young art student was also surprised that some of his professors did not even know the name of a leading painter of the day who was widely discussed in the art journals that Dalí followed so closely.

There were also personal reasons for Dalí's desire to put Madrid behind him. The Spanish capital had come to symbolize not only the lack of seriousness about art he felt in the institute; it also represented his own failings. However much Dalí might scorn conventionality, he did feel that he had at times lived a wasteful life in Madrid. Paris, by contrast, seemed to him a healthy and stimulating place to live. In Paris, he believed, art was not something one read about in newspapers—it was a way of life. In Paris, the legendary Pablo Picasso painted, and daring poets and writers were striving to bring about a total revolution in art. Dalí was sure that the art world of Paris would embrace him—if only he could get there.

Dalí packed his luggage and started to leave his room, but then he hesitated. Somehow it seemed out of place to carry his old possessions back home to Figueres—where he knew he would soon have to confront his furious and disappointed father—when he was trying to rid himself of his entire way of life. Realizing this, he simply left his baggage in his room and proceeded to the railroad station with only the clothes on his back. After purchasing his ticket to Figueres, he noticed an old beggar woman nearby. He walked over to a flower vendor, purchased a bouquet of gardenias with the last of his money, and presented the flowers to the surprised beggar. Somehow it seemed an appropriate gesture before the long journey home to face his father.

# CHAPTER
## T W O

# THE SEEDS OF AMBITION

S alvador Dalí i Domènech was born on the morning of May 11, 1904, in Figueres, a small city tucked away in the northeast corner of Spain, a mere 15 miles from the French border. His birth was an especially joyous event because his parents' first child, also named Salvador, had died nine months earlier, bringing the Dalí family much sorrow. Delighted to have a child in the house again, his parents made young Salvador the center of their attention. Three years later, Salvador gained a younger sister when his mother gave birth to a daughter, who was christened Ana María.

From all outward appearances, Salvador's childhood might have been expected to be happy and contented. Figueres was a quiet, secluded place during his early years, and the Dalís lived in comfort. Salvador Dalí senior earned a considerable income, serving as one of only five local notaries. (In Spain, the profession of notary is highly respected; notaries have degrees in law and act as signatories in financial and inheritance matters.)

Still, the Dalís' much-loved son was subject to fits of extreme rage and a variety of childhood ailments that seemed to have no physical cause. He drove his father from the dinner table with self-induced coughing fits and wet his bed until he was eight years old. Salvador could also be cruel to other children. He

*The Dalí family enjoys an outing on the Empordàn coast. The family was prosperous and well-respected, but conflicts between Salvador's parents and the haunting memory of a family tragedy created serious tensions beneath the surface.*

21

once deliberately kicked his sister in the head. On another occasion, he caused one of his playmates to fall from a considerable height, resulting in a serious injury.

Just below the surface of the happy and loving Dalí family, there were disturbing elements. The most important was the lingering impact of the first Salvador Dalí's death. There is reason to believe that the parents never recovered from this tragedy; consequently, the event had a powerful effect on the life of their second son.

The influence of his dead brother permeated young Salvador's environment. He had to play with his brother's toys and games, and his parents spoke incessantly about the first Salvador. Salvador was terrified by a picture of his brother that the Dalís kept in their bedroom. He became obsessed with the idea that it was his body lying under the earth, decomposing. His mother often took Salvador to visit his brother's grave, and it disturbed him greatly to see his own name inscribed on the headstone. As Meredith Etherington-Smith wrote in her biography of Dalí, *The Persistence of Memory,* "Dalí's extreme egocentricity must have certainly stemmed from these constant reminders of the 'other' Salvador. He was fighting early on to prove that he existed." Dalí himself later took note of this problem when he wrote, "At the age of six I wanted to be a cook. At seven I wanted to be Napoleon."

The family atmosphere was further complicated by the differences between Salvador's parents. They were extreme opposites in temperament and outlook, and this created tension in the household. Dalí's father, an atheist with an angry, domineering personality, forgave none of his son's misbehavior; his mother, a devout Catholic, forgave all. Not surprisingly, Salvador had a very stormy relationship with his father and adored his mother. While Salvador's reactions to his environment may seem exaggerated, all accounts agree that he was an unusually sensitive child who suffered deep emotional conflicts.

Beyond his family environment, Salvador's character and future artwork were influenced by his native province of Catalonia, and in particular the region known as the Empordà, where Figueres is located. One of Spain's most vital and important provinces, Catalonia extends along Spain's northeast coast, bordering the Mediterranean Sea. At various times in its past, Catalonia has been an independent nation with a rich history of trade and culture, as well as its own language, Catalan, which is still in use today. Catalans thus have a strong sense of their own identity and achievements, especially in the world of the arts.

The easternmost part of Catalonia, the Empordà, is bounded by the Pyrenees Mountains on the north and the Albera hills on the south. Between these hills and mountains is a barren plain that is remarkable for its flatness. Dalí would later describe it as "the most objective piece of landscape that exists in the world." Within this flat expanse, the Albera hills seem to arise so abruptly out of nowhere as to appear unreal, creating a haunting landscape that would often appear in the adult Dalí's canvases.

Each summer of Salvador's childhood was spent at Cadaqués, a nearby fishing village. There, too, Salvador found himself in a unique and fantastic landscape. Situated on an extremely rocky coastline, Cadaqués is a windy place marked by violent climatic changes. The *tramontana,* a cold wind, blows from the north for almost nine months of the year. It has been known to unnerve local inhabitants, causing many suicides. The winds have helped carve the huge rocks along the edge of the sea into strange shapes. When young Salvador was taken for boat trips up the coast, he would spy these rocks, and they reminded him of human or animal shapes. (Their shapes had inspired the local fishermen to name them, creating a local mythology: the Monk, the Anvil, and the Lion's Head were some examples.) Salvador noticed how the shapes of the rocks changed as the boat moved past them, suggesting to his mind still other images.

*A view of Cadaqués, the fishing village where the Dalí family spent their summer vacations. The striking rock formations along the coastline and the peculiar ways of the village's residents made a lasting impression on the young Salvador, influencing both his art and his behavior.*

In keeping with its strange landscape, the town did not lack for colorful characters. There was Josep Barrera, a local smuggler, and Noi de Tona, a tramp who pulled teeth for a living. Of all the residents of the little port city, it was Lidia Nogueres who made the deepest impression on young Salvador. A woman with a deep

and elemental connection with the earth and the sea, Nogueres was the widow of a fisherman who had drowned in the Mediterranean's blue waters, leaving her with two slow-witted sons. She completely dominated her sons, and there is evidence that she may have had an incestuous relationship with both of them. It is not to be wondered at, then, that the people of Cadaqués commonly believed her to be a witch. But if Nogueres had a dark side, she was also enthusiastic about art, and she would one day play a crucial role in Salvador's life.

Cadaqués also provided the link between young Salvador and the world of art by bringing him into contact with the Pitxots. A wealthy and accomplished Catalan family, the Pitxots practically constituted a local art movement all by themselves. Ramón Pitxot was a painter associated with Picasso. Lluís, one of Ramón's brothers, played the violin; a sister, María Pitxot de Gay, a famous opera singer, was especially renowned for singing the title role in Georges Bizet's *Carmen*; another brother, Ricardo, was an accomplished cellist and a favorite pupil of one of the 20th century's greatest musicians, Pablo Casals. The three musical siblings performed concerts together for King Alfonso XIII. Pepito, another brother, besides being a lawyer, was an expert gardener and photographer and had even decorated the family's vacation home at Cadaqués.

The Pitxots entertained friends from all over Europe at Cadaqués, and they also displayed the unconventional behavior that seemed to distinguish those lured by the small Spanish port. On one outing, members of the family played classical music by the Mediterranean in order to have a dialogue with the sea, and Ricardo especially loved to take his cello outside and perform for flocks of turkeys. On some especially beautiful, clear nights, Salvador was amazed to see Lluís and Ricardo take their stringed instruments out to a boat anchored in front of their house and play Mozart airs, while bobbing up and down on the waves.

As Salvador grew older, his behavior seemed to become equally odd. One day, his father sent him to buy some tortillas. When Salvador returned, he gave his father two rolls. "And the tortillas, where are they?" his father demanded. "I got rid of them," Salvador replied nonchalantly. "And why did you get rid of them?" "Because I didn't like the yellow." When Salvador senior recounted this incident to a friend, he said, "I have a son who pays not the slightest heed to reality; he doesn't know what a five-centimo piece is. . . . He has no idea, you realize; he's a hopeless case. How will all this end?"

At about age seven, Salvador began attending school. Because of his atheism and liberal political views, Salvador senior refused to send his son to the school that all the city's more prosperous residents used, for it was run by Marist priests. Instead, the boy had to attend the free school where the city's poor children went and where there would supposedly be no religious influence.

Life in the public school was miserable for Salvador. His mother dressed him in fine clothes, including a sailor suit, shoes with silver buttons, and to top it all off, a cane with a dog's-head handle made of silver. His appearance could not have made a greater contrast with that of his classmates, who wore discarded clothes and sometimes went barefoot. Not surprisingly, the other children bullied him terribly.

This new wound to Salvador's sensitive nature may have been slight compared with that inflicted by the school's strange atmosphere. The school's teacher, S. D. Esteban Trayter, created the unhealthy ambience. Trayter's appearance was grotesque: he had a white beard that was so long it almost reached the ground. As if that were not strange enough, Trayter parted his beard in the middle and wove each section into plaits. Constantly indulging in snuff, a powder made of ground tobacco, Trayter made his bizarre facial ornamentation truly disgusting by sneezing snuff into it.

Behind the classroom, Trayter had a room in which he kept a collection of very strange objects, some of them apparently pieces of medical equipment, and their unknown use made Salvador shudder. Trayter also had a mummified frog that he called his "dancing girl" because of the way he could make it jerk about at the end of a string. Dalí later recalled that the elderly teacher would take him back into this strange room, sit him on his lap, and stroke his chin. One of Dalí's biographers, considering the painter's lifelong aversion to being touched, has speculated that Trayter may have done more than stroke Salvador's chin.

Whatever torments Salvador endured during his one year at the public school, it was around this time that he first began to paint, perhaps influenced by Ramón Pitxot's example. Salvador's aunt had a millinery shop, and she gave him hatbox covers that became his first canvases. There were two laundry rooms on the top floor of the Dalí home, and Salvador asked to use one for his painting. The request was granted, and the laundry room became his first studio.

Noticing his son's interest in painting, the elder Dalí gave Salvador a collection of books on great artists. Salvador carried the volumes up to his laundry room—studio—its walls by then covered with painted hatbox tops—and on hot days he would take long baths in a laundry tub, leisurely studying the world's greatest paintings.

Not surprisingly, Salvador learned nothing during his year at Trayter's school. Abandoning his political principles, Salvador senior finally enrolled his son in the Marist school. But there, too, Salvador paid scant attention to his studies, spending most of his time gazing out the window at a pair of cypress trees. He did not pass on to the next grade.

Eventually, Salvador fell ill, no doubt because of the severe stress on his young mind. When he was finally well enough to get out of bed, the family doctor recommended that Salvador spend some time in the country. Pepito Pitxot, the family lawyer, kindly offered the use of the Pitxot family manor. Salvador enjoyed resting in the manor's shady garden, but what really captured his attention was Ramón Pitxot's paintings, which were done in the styles of impressionism and pointillism, two closely related schools of painting. Many of the canvases hung in the manor's dining room. They were such a revelation to Salvador that he became totally absorbed by them, spilling his breakfast coffee onto his shirt time and again as he studied the paintings.

Inspired by Pitxot's work, he decided to paint a still life of cherries. He found a worm-eaten door leaning against the wall of a granary to serve as his canvas. Salvador set to work, using only three colors—white and two different shades of red—and applied the oil paints directly from the tubes, without using a brush. When the painting was done, Salvador showed it to Pitxot, who pointed out that he had not painted the cherries' stems. Salvador then ate some of the cherries and glued their stems onto the door. Struck by Salvador's on-the-spot creativity and by the effort he had put into the painting, Pitxot said he would talk to his father about arranging for Salvador to take drawing lessons. Salvador immediately replied that he did not need drawing lessons as he was an impressionist. (The impressionist painters of the 19th century, such as Paul Cézanne and Vincent Van Gogh, used daubs of paint to capture the "impression" of objects

*After a traumatic childhood, painting and drawing offered release and consolation for Dalí.*
Self-Portrait in the Studio, Cadaqués, *painted around 1919, shows how strongly Dalí's early*
*work was influenced by the impressionist paintings of his friend Ramón Pitxot.*

rather than rendering them in exact detail.) While this response gave Pitxot a hearty laugh, he insisted on the necessity of the lessons.

When Salvador was well enough to return to Figueres, he began to take classes in the evening with Joan Núñez, an accomplished artist who had won the prestigious Prix de Rome award in engraving. Salvador, now 12 years old, respected Núñez a great deal and took the artist's instructions very seriously. Salvador had a great talent for drawing, and under Núñez's direction he developed this gift until he became, in the words of one of his biographers, "one of the finest draftsmen of the twentieth century."

Salvador began to paint continually. Some of his first paintings were of landscapes around Figueres; others were quiet domestic scenes, often portraying female relatives sewing. He soon began to experiment, applying the paint to canvases in very thick layers in order to create a texture on the surface. Attempting to render depth of light, he began to stick stones onto the canvases and to paint over them. In a painting of a sunset, Salvador used stones to represent the clouds in the sky. His father liked the painting and hung it in the dining room. When the stones would occasionally drop off the painting and hit the sideboard below, the elder Dalí would calmly say, "Nothing but stones falling from our child's sky."

With the approach of adolescence, Salvador began to dress in a more individualistic way. He grew his hair and sideburns long, wore a huge ascot tie, and carried about a meerschaum pipe, the bowl of which had been carved into the face of an Arab with a broad grin. As Salvador's behavior became more eccentric, his classmates delighted all the more in being cruel to him. When they found out he was so terrified of grasshoppers that the mere sight of them would throw him into fits of violent hysteria, they brought grass-

*Constantly experimenting, Dalí quickly moved away from his early impressionistic style, as can be seen in this 1921 self-portrait. Here Dalí self-consciously portrays himself as an artist, with a pipe and a floppy black hat.*

hoppers into the classroom to provoke Salvador. Under the circumstances, it is not surprising that he was not a dedicated student; although he remained at the Marist school until he was 15, he paid attention only in drawing class.

After leaving the Marist school, Salvador enrolled in the General and Technical Institute, where he studied for the *batxillerat,* the equivalent of a high school diploma. The school must have awakened a studious impulse in him, because he eventually graduated with extremely high grades. Perhaps what he had needed most of all was to get away from both the strictness of the Marist school and the intolerance of his fellow students.

At the institute, Salvador's talents began to unfold in several directions. He started to keep a journal in which he recorded his thoughts, a lifelong habit that would eventually provide the raw material for the books he would write. In 1919, he and two of his schoolmates created a magazine, which they named *Studium*. In its pages, Salvador wrote at length about the great classical painters. His diary from this period shows that he was becoming better adjusted socially. He made a number of new friends, played soccer, and began to show an interest in girls.

Salvador's greatest achievement in 1919 was, no doubt, the first exhibition of his work. The local exhibition featured art by 30 painters. When an art critic reviewed the show, he singled out Salvador's work for special comment: "Let us speak about Mr. Salvador Dalí Domènech. The man who has within him what the paintings he has exhibited in the salon of the Concert Society reveal to us already has great artistic talent. . . . Salvador Dalí Domènech will be a great painter."

Perhaps it was praise such as this that convinced Salvador's father not to oppose his son's determination to be a painter. After some inquiries, Salvador senior decided to send his son to Madrid's San Fernando Institute of Fine Arts. Salvador, no doubt, welcomed the decision, knowing that he could now devote himself completely to the study of art. Given his rebellious nature, he must have looked forward to being on his own for the first time. However, just three months before he was scheduled to take his entrance examinations for the San Fernando Institute, his mother died of cancer. The loss was extremely painful for the sensitive youth. He later wrote, "I had to achieve glory to avenge the affront caused me by the death of my mother, whom I adored religiously."

The intense artistic atmosphere he would find in Madrid would offer him just the preparation he needed for glory.

# MADRID

In May 1921, accompanied by his father and sister, Dalí journeyed to Madrid to take the entrance examination for the San Fernando Institute of Fine Arts. The entrance test was to make a drawing of a sculpture of the god Bacchus by the Renaissance sculptor Jacopo Sansovino. Dalí had six days in which to finish the drawing, and the institute's rules stated that the completed work must be of a precise size. Dalí threw himself into the task. Whether due to nervousness or a failure to understand the examination requirements, when Dalí finished the drawing on the sixth day he suddenly realized that his work was too small. Both he and his father were horrified, but there was no time to start over, so he submitted the drawing as it was. The drawing lessons that Dalí had taken with Joan Núñez had paid off handsomely: impressed by the extremely high quality of Dalí's work, the examining committee approved the drawing in spite of its dimensions and admitted Dalí to the institute.

Dalí senior believed that many artists led reckless and irresponsible lives, and he wanted to do all that he could to protect his son from the dangers of such wayward living. After some investigation, he enrolled Salvador in the Residencia de Estudiantes, feeling that it would be a safe environment. The Resi—as the students who lived there generally referred to it—had been founded in 1910 by Alberto Jiménez Fraúd, a liberal professor who wished to model Spain's educational system on that of England. Fraúd believed that

*When Dalí moved to Madrid to study art, his genuine originality soon became evident. Still, it would be several years before his talent would mature, allowing him to fully express his own highly personal vision of the world.*

35

by creating a residence where students would be exposed to the best of both the arts and the sciences he could ensure that they would become cultured and well rounded.

The Residencia was a cluster of five buildings that were designed to offer a complete learning environment. Besides a dormitory and dining hall, it provided a modest laboratory and an excellent modern library. In addition, the Residencia even published books. Apparently impressed by Fraúd's idealism, some of the century's greatest thinkers came to speak at the Residencia: among them were the German physicist Albert Einstein, the French scientist Marie Curie, the English novelist H. G. Wells, and the English economist John Maynard Keynes. Poets and writers would often stay overnight at the Residencia and visit with the students, and the groundbreaking theories of the Austrian physician Sigmund Freud were also widely discussed by the Residencia's occupants.

Dalí entered the Residencia in September 1921. Even in this tolerant and open atmosphere, he managed to make an impression with his very first entrance into the dining hall: Dalí's long hair and sideburns, long cape that swept the floor, baggy pants, and other affectations caused the other Residencia students to whisper to one another about his strange appearance.

Exhibitionistic tendencies aside, Dalí had come to the institute to learn, and he went to his classes eager for instruction. He was quickly disappointed. The Resi may have been open to the latest intellectual and artistic currents, but the San Fernando Institue was not. Dalí was amazed to find his professors enthralled by impressionism, an art movement whose apogee had passed over 40 years earlier. It had been over 10 years since Picasso and Georges Braque had started the movement known as cubism, yet Dali's instructors

*Long hair and flowing ties were among the trademarks of Dalí (bottom left in this 1925 photograph) during his student years at the San Fernando Institute. Although Dalí found inspiration among his classmates, he discovered to his dismay that the institute itself was artistically backward.*

had not even heard of it. (The cubists abandoned any attempt to portray objects in their everyday appearance; instead, they broke everything down into planes and surfaces and arranged these elements on their canvases in new and sometimes startling combinations.) The professors' ignorance of and disinterest in what was happening in the rest of Europe must have seemed especially strange to Dalí because a number of Spanish painters—Joan Miró and Juan Gris, for example, in addition to Picasso—had made significant contributions to contemporary painting and art theory.

Even worse, from Dalí's point of view, was the professors' indifference to classical technique, which even the impressionists had always respected. The only professor Dalí found at the institute who taught in the old manner was José Carbonero, a drawing instructor who had taught Picasso, but Dalí found to his chagrin that Carbonero was not respected.

"The pupils laughed at him," Dalí wrote—"at his coat, the black pearl stickpin he wore in his tie, and his white gloves. His skill was unmatched, but no sooner did he turn his back than the little upstarts erased his corrections, which in fact reflected the gifts of a true master. I preferred to keep apart from that bunch of loafers and idiots, and go on with my Cubist experiments."

Ironically, because of Dalí's interest in technique, his professors thought that he did not have the makings of an artist: they thought that art was based on feeling. Never one to be easily discouraged, Dalí decided that if the San Fernando Institute of Fine Arts would not teach him about technique and the old masters, he would learn about them on his own. Dalí painted in his room at night and whenever he could during the day, working for long hours at a stretch. When he was not painting, he read his Italian and French art magazines and visited Madrid's famous Prado Museum, seeking inspiration in the canvases of the world's greatest painters.

Dalí's interest in everything that was new in art brought him together with two fellow students who would rank among the century's great artists—Luis Buñuel and Federico García Lorca. There were various cliques of students in the Residencia, and one of these was the avant-garde literary and artistic group that included Buñuel and Lorca. (The term *avant-garde,* French for "advance guard," is used to describe artists, writers, and musicians who are at the forefront of developing new forms and techniques.) These students had been strongly influenced by the dadaist movement. Dada, a reaction to World War I (1914–18), in which the so-called civilized nations had killed 30 million of one another's citizens, particularly suited the mood of these students because it had declared war on both morality and taste. The theory of dadaism was that conventional values supported and were part of a corrupt social system that resulted in such horrors

*Disappointed with his art instructors, Dalí spent many hours seeking inspiration in Madrid's Prado Museum. Among his favorite paintings was Hieronymous Bosch's* Garden of Earthly Delights, *a 16th-century masterpiece that influenced Dalí's later work.*

as World War I. The rebellious young Spaniards also admired a movement known as futurism, which tried to express in the arts the dynamism of the new machines that were coming into use during the early 20th century.

For all their cries against conformity, the group's members did have their own mode of dress, wearing British tweeds and trimming their hair in the style of the 19th-century British dandy Beau Brummel. Dalí soon discarded his own quirky style of dress for that favored by his new friends. They also taught him how to drink and where to be seen. Over the next few years, the youths spent much of their parents' money in the Ritz and Palace hotels and the more fashionable Madrid bars, such as Rector's. One of their more amusing activities was the Noble Order of Toledo, organized by Buñuel after he became fascinated by the ancient Spanish city. To join the order, a student had to love Toledo unconditionally, get drunk there, and while drunk, wander the streets for an entire night in quest of adventure.

While there was certainly no shortage of high spirits, personality, and talent among this group of

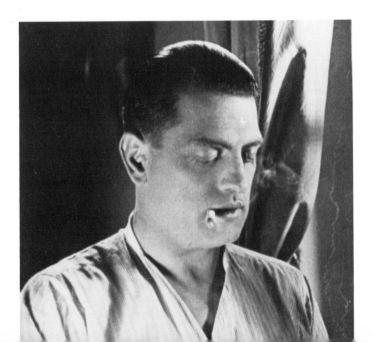

*The Spanish filmmaker Luis Buñuel, pictured here during the 1920s, was one of the lively and original spirits Dalí met during his student days. Dalí and Buñuel later collaborated on one of the most unusual works in film history.*

friends, it was equally clear that Lorca outshone the rest. Gifted with a winning personality and diverse talents, Lorca easily made friends. Buñuel wrote that he was "brilliant and charming. . . . With his dark, shining eyes, he had a magnetism that few could resist." Lorca could easily gain everyone's affection and admiration through reciting poetry, singing, performing magic tricks, and telling stories, in addition to his gift for conversation. Dalí soon succumbed to the poet's charm, later writing that "the personality of Federico García Lorca produced an immense impression on me."

By the time Dalí was in his second year at Madrid, he had become so thoroughly disenchanted with his professors that he helped foment a rebellion against them. The trouble began when a vacancy occurred on the institute's faculty. Candidates for the position were required to submit two paintings, and all the entries were displayed together. Dalí went to see the exhibition with some fellow members of the avant-garde set. They agreed that all the canvases were poor, with the exception of those painted by one particular candidate. Rumors circulated that institutional politics rather than artistic ability would determine who was hired. When the decision was announced at an assembly and the winner was not the candidate preferred by the avant-garde group, Dalí immediately rose and left the room. After he left, a riot began as students yelled insults and threw objects at the tribunal. The police were called as the demonstration spilled out into the street.

The institute, greatly upset by the riot, could not single out anyone to make an example of, as the protest had not been planned. Still, Dalí's abruptly leaving the assembly was taken by some faculty members as a signal to start the riot. Dalí was summoned and asked to name students who had taken part in the demonstration. He refused and was suspended for one year, without any guarantee that he would ever be permitted to return.

Dalí's father was furious. He sent Tieta, his second wife and former sister-in-law, to Madrid so that he could get a reliable report on the situation. She wrote him an optimistic letter, saying that Dalí's work was greatly admired and that there was a good possibility that Dalí would be permitted to return to the institute after a year. Dalí's father finally got over his fury, and the family came to feel that Dalí had been treated unfairly. Dalí returned to Figueres to spend the year of suspension.

In 1923, the year that Dalí was suspended from the institute, Spanish general Miguel Primo de Rivera dismissed the Cortes, Spain's representative assembly, and established a dictatorship. After Catalan separatists staged an unsuccessful revolt, the entire province of Catalonia seethed with unrest. In May 1924, when Dalí's father tried to fulfill his role as an election official, the Guardia Civil, Spain's national police force, prevented him from doing so and threatened to kill him. They showed him a list that they had compiled, naming people whom they might arrest, and the name at the top of the list was his son's. The dictatorship was no doubt unhappy that a state notary did not hide his sympathy for the Catalan movement for independence, nor was it pleased that the notary's son was the only person in Figueres to subscribe to the French Communist newspaper *L'Humanité*.

Not long after his father was shown the list, Dalí was arrested. In jail, Dalí demanded to see the prison governor. When asked the reason for his request, Dalí replied that viewing the governor's decorations and sword would be a welcome diversion. Dalí remained in jail until June, when a partial amnesty was declared.

Dalí spent the following summer at Cadaqués, painting and taking drawing lessons from Joan Núñez,

*Poet and playwright Federico García Lorca (left) joined Dalí on vacation in 1925 at Cadaqués. Endowed with seemingly boundless charm and talent, Lorca was on the verge of world fame when he and Dali visited Cadaqués. During the vacation the poet fell in love with Dalí and wrote one of his greatest poems, "Ode to Salvador Dalí," soon afterward.*

his former teacher. When autumn came and Dalí still was not allowed to attend the institute, he returned to the Residencia and was greeted as a hero for having been a political prisoner. So as not to waste his time until he could reenroll, he took drawing lessons at another school and spent much time reading, particularly Freud's *Interpretation of Dreams,* which offered startling theories on the unconscious workings of the human mind.

As time passed, Dalí and Lorca became closer and closer, until Dalí invited Lorca to spend Holy Week of 1925 with his family in Cadaqués. By all accounts, this vacation was a magical one for both young men. Dalí showed Lorca all his favorite places in Cadaqués, sites that had held special significance for the young artist since his childhood. He took the poet on boat trips to see the strange rocks that altered their shapes as the viewer's vantage point changed, and also introduced Lorca to Lidia Nogueres, the reputed witch. Her mind now gone, Nogueres produced an astonishing babble of fantasies. Lorca was so taken with the madwoman that for the rest of his life he would keep a photograph of her on his piano. Dalí also took Lorca to see the famed ruins of Empúrias, the Greek and Roman trading port from which the Empordà took its name. There, Lorca saw an ancient mosaic that so moved him that he was inspired to write a poem about it. In general, Lorca was entranced by the beauty of Cadaqués.

The Dalí family was just as impressed with Lorca as Lorca was with the Empordà. One evening, Dalí encouraged Lorca to read aloud a play that he had just finished writing, *Mariana Pineda*. By the end of the reading, Dalí's father was so deeply moved that he could not help exclaiming that Lorca was the cen-

*Pablo Picasso's 1921 painting* The Three Musicians *shows the influence of cubism. When Dalí met Picasso in Paris, he was deeply influenced by his fellow Spaniard, who had almost single-handedly changed the course of 20th-century art.*

tury's greatest poet. Lorca continued to mesmerize and charm the family with impromptu performances of various kinds: mimicry, poetry recitals, singing, anecdotes, and the creative, symbolic acts of a poet. For example, one morning Lorca entered the Dalí household holding a branch of coral he had found. He told Dalí's sister that it was blood from veins that had solidified. The young poet then placed the coral in the hand of a statue of the Virgin Mary.

Dalí spent the days painting, while Lorca wrote. In this idyllic atmosphere, it is hardly surprising that Lorca, being homosexual, fell in love with Dalí. Dalí, having similar feelings for Lorca, began the first of many paintings and drawings he would do of his friend.

After the vacation, Lorca returned to Madrid and began a poem based on the wonderful week that had just ended. Entitled "Ode to Salvador Dalí," it is considered one of the poet's greatest works. A few verses from it capture Dalí as he was beginning to come into his own:

> O Salvador Dalí, with an olive-smooth voice,
> I'll speak of what your person and pictures speak to
>     me.
> No praise for your imperfect adolescent brush,
>     but rather sing of the perfect path of your arrows.
> I'll sing your beautiful effects with Catalan lights,
>     and your love for all that is explicable.
> I'll sing your tender, astronomic heart,
>     your card-game heart, a heart without wounds.

If Lorca drew inspiration from Dalí, Dalí was, in turn, stimulated by his friend's company. He was working feverishly to prepare for an exhibition in Madrid. In addition, he had been using the period of his suspension to write for two important publications, *Gaceta de los Artes* (Art Gazette), published in Barcelona, and *L'Amic des Arts* (The Friend of the

Arts), published in Sitges. Josép Dalmau, the owner of
an art gallery in Barcelona, had read Dalí's writings
and had been impressed enough to offer Dalí a one-
man show. Realizing that this was a golden opportunity, Dalí worked like a demon.

By the time the show took place in November,
Dalí had completed 5 drawings and 17 paintings.
Catalan critics gave the show a very warm reception,
with one of them writing, "Rarely does a young
painter appear with so much aplomb as this Salvador
Dalí, child of Figueres." Responding to others who
noted the great influence of the French avant-garde
on Dalí, the critic went on to say, "If Salvador Dalí has
turned his face toward France, it is because he can do
it, because the gifts for becoming a painter that God
gave him must have time to ripen."

Perhaps in response to this kind of praise, Dalí's
father offered him the present of a vacation abroad
during Holy Week of 1926. Dalí stopped in Paris on
his way to Brussels, Belgium, for he had secured an
invitation to meet the great Picasso. Arriving at Picasso's studio, Dalí told the master, "I have come to see
you before visiting the Louvre [Paris's great art mu-
seum]." "You're quite right," Picasso replied immod-
estly. Picasso showed Dalí his paintings, one after
another, without saying a word. Finally, Picasso gave
Dalí a look that the young artist interpreted to mean,
"You get the idea?" Dalí's expression conveyed the
response, "I get it!"

Dalí finally learned that he would be allowed to
reenroll at the San Fernando Institute in the fall of
1925. When he returned to Madrid, he found Lorca
back at the Residencia. Though Dalí and Lorca had
kept in constant touch by letter, over one year had
elapsed since they had last seen each other during
their Cadaqués vacation. There is evidence that Lorca
may have now urged Dalí to embark on a full-fledged

*Dalí painted his* Still Life: Sandía *in 1924, while he was suspended from the San Fernando Institute. The painting was strongly influenced by cubism; before long, Dalí was painting canvases that were even more experimental.*

love affair and that Dalí finally drew back from this step. Most of Dalí's biographers agree that he had a significant homosexual component in his personality, but on the whole, he appears to have repressed these feelings or channeled them into work and various friendships.

Having seen the lights of Paris firsthand, and having been offered a second exhibition by Dalmau, Dalí by now certainly did turn his face toward France. Spain seemed more and more a backwater of the art world, and by this time the institute appeared almost a joke to him. He felt that he had to get to France immediately, no matter what the cost. The best way to do this, it seemed to Dalí, was to make a clean break with the institute, which he accomplished by getting himself expelled. Without the safety net of a degree, he had to rely solely on his talent.

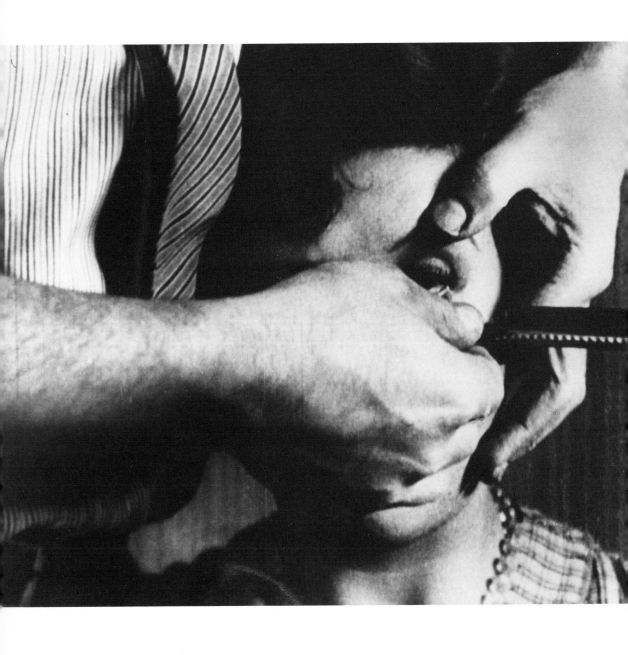

# THE SHOCK
# OF THE NEW

During the summer of 1926, Dalí returned to Figueres to confront an enraged father and unsympathetic family. From his father's point of view, Dalí had thrown away an opportunity for a brilliant career. Needless to say, when Dalí asked for money to go to Paris, his father refused. It would take three long years of hard work before Dalí would again set foot in the French capital.

Still, there was reason for Dalí to hope for better days. During the summer, Joan Miró visited Cadaqués and brought along his Paris art dealer, Pierre Loeb. Miró and Loeb wanted to see Dalí's paintings. A month later, Dalí received a letter from Loeb. Instead of making an offer to represent Dalí, however, Loeb merely asked Dalí to remain in touch. Loeb suggested that when Dalí's work was more mature, he might be interested in representing him. Though Dalí's paintings and writings had made an impression on the larger art world, it was not ready to embrace him.

Thrown back on his own resources, Dalí was forced to create his own philosophy of art and determine the values by which he would live and create. He began to move away from the classical style into a new direction of his own. One of the first canvases that shows a new aesthetic is *Still Life by Moonlight,* in which a severed head, combining Dalí's and Lorca's

*Film audiences were shocked and outraged when Buñuel and Dalí's* Un chien andalou *opened with the image of an eye slit open by a razor blade. Like all of surrealist art, the film was an attempt to portray the purely irrational side of life. "NOTHING, in the film," wrote Buñuel "SYMBOLIZES ANYTHING."*

faces, lies on a moonlit table. Also on the table are a guitar, several fish, a fishing net, and an artist's palette. In a letter to an art critic, written around this time, Dalí stated his philosophy. He explained his lack of religious feeling but denied that this meant he had no feelings at all. On the contrary, he said, it was "precisely the absolute absence of religious instinct and the inner world that led me . . . toward a passion for the exterior world. . . . *Things have no significance outside their strict objectivity* and it is in this that their miraculous poetry dwells." Dalí would continue for many years to explore the poetry that he found in everyday objects.

In October 1926, Dalí exhibited *Still Life by Moonlight* and another painting in a show in Barcelona. When his second exhibition at the Dalmau Gallery came in December 1926, more of his experimental canvases were shown. One painting from the show, sold to the Pittsburgh Museum of Modern Art, was an exquisite example of the poetry that can be found in everyday objects. In this work, *Basket of Bread,* Dalí's technical virtuosity—the result of those hard-earned skills that his former professors had sneered at— enabled him to make an ordinary basket of bread appear magical and mystical by the masterful use of light, for the bread seems to glow with a luminescence of its own.

The exhibition was a considerable success: every painting was sold. Following the show, Dalí again approached his father for money to go to Paris. Again, his father refused. Still, Dalí was beginning to lay a foundation for independence. It also appears certain that Dalí's artistic breakthroughs were stimulated by his friendship with Lorca. Indeed, there was so much contact between the two men during this time that the period between 1926 and 1928 has been called Dalí's "Lorca years."

*Dalí works in his studio in 1934.* Life by Moonlight, *hanging on the wall at the extreme left, marked the transition from Dalí's earlier paintings to his later surrealist works.*

In the summer of 1927, while Lorca was in Catalonia, Dalí began a painting, whose original title, *The Forest of Gadgets,* had been suggested by the poet. This work was the first of Dalí's canvases to be influenced by surrealism, an artistic style that seeks to draw images directly from the subconscious mind, reproducing the haunting atmosphere of dreams. In the painting, Lorca's head, half-buried in sand on a beach, casts a shadow that turns out to be Dalí's. A dead donkey lies nearby, infested with flies. Also nearby are a severed arm, a decapitated female dummy, another severed head, and another rotting corpse. A strange

triangular "gadget" stands upright on the beach. The painting's final title, *Honey Is Sweeter Than Blood,* was taken from a phrase of Lidia Nogueres's.

The theories of Sigmund Freud exerted a great deal of influence on Dalí's venture into surrealism. Freud stated that the mind has two main divisions, the conscious and the subconscious. The subconscious is so named because one is not directly aware of it: it lies, so to speak, "beneath" the everyday, waking mind. For this reason, the subconscious reveals itself in symbolic images and actions, such as dreams, mythology, and the actions of those who are classified as mentally ill. The subconscious also contains thoughts and feelings that are blocked from the mind because they are considered inappropriate. Freud placed great emphasis on the sexual nature of subconscious impulses, believing that most people's anxieties stemmed from unresolved sexual conflicts. It followed then that people could become well adjusted by examining their true sexual feelings—no matter how fiercely condemned by society—and by accepting them (although this did not necessarily mean acting upon those feelings).

In the fall of 1927, Dalí wrote to Lorca that the new style of painting was giving him a great sense of relief: "Federico, I am painting pictures which make me die for joy, I am creating with an absolute naturalness, without the slightest aesthetic concern, I am making things that inspire me with a very profound emotion and I am trying to paint them honestly." *Honey Is Sweeter Than Blood* is typical of Dalí's more mature work. He once said that throughout his life he painted the same picture over and over again. It was Dalí's way of saying that he would always work with the elemental themes of sexuality and death as seen through the prism of his own personal experience and thus usually set in his own visual frame of reference, the Empordàn plain and coast.

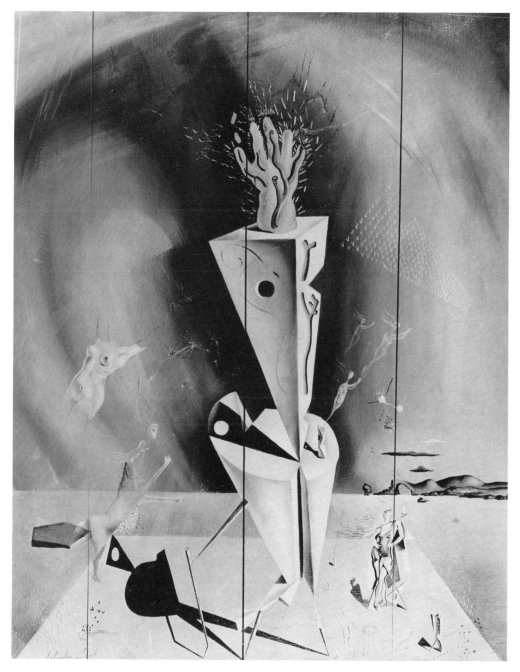

*Similar in both style and content to the badly damaged* Honey Is Sweeter Than Blood, *the* 1925 *painting* Apparatus and Hand *shows Dalí beginning to move firmly into the surrealist camp and developing his own personal style.*

In 1927, Lorca vacationed again with the Dalís in Cadaqués, this time for two months. For all the shared creativity, artistic excitement, and romantic feelings that existed between Dalí and Lorca, a difference in their temperaments was already in evidence. Although Dalí had a great respect for the artists of the past, he wanted to portray the present world from a modern point of view. Lorca was from the province of Andalusia in southern Spain, and he drew much of his inspiration from the region's folk songs and traditions. Dalí began to feel that Lorca was living in the past, and he urged his friend not to ignore the modern world.

Dalí had stayed in touch with Buñuel as well as Lorca, and Buñuel soon grew jealous of Lorca and Dalí's closeness. His jealousy was aggravated by his strong prejudice against homosexuality. He soon determined to drive a wedge between the two men and did everything in his power to turn Dalí against Lorca. As it happened, the rupture between the two men came about rather more easily than Buñuel might have expected. Buñuel was in Paris, trying to get a foot in the door of the film world, and in November 1927 he was put in charge of the film sections of two publications. He immediately published an essay that Dalí had written on film. Dalí began to feel that if he had to choose between Buñuel and Lorca, Buñuel would be the winner. The filmmaker was in Paris, which was where Dalí wanted to be. Moreover, Buñuel shared Dalí's aggressive enthusiasm for the modern.

In 1927, Dalí threw in his lot with surrealism, a decision he had been heading toward for some time. The word *surrealism,* meaning "super real" or "beyond real," had been coined by the French poet Guillaume Apollinaire in 1917. Surrealism grew out of the dada movement, which had used ridicule and nonsense to attack the false values of a bankrupt society. André

Breton, a French poet who had been a member of the dada group, organized the surrealist movement in 1924. In his *Surrealist Manifesto,* Breton wrote that surrealism was "pure psychic automatism, by which it is intended to express verbally, in writing or in any other way, the true process of thought. It is the dictation of thought, free from the exercise of reason, and every aesthetic or moral preoccupation." In other words, the purpose of the movement was to free artists from the inhibitions of the rational mind so that they might have access to the riches held in the subconscious.

To achieve this, the surrealists attacked with considerable gusto any and all cherished rules and values, whether cultural or artistic. At its best, surrealism was an act of faith in the power of the imagination to revitalize art and to free the human spirit. Much of the best work of the surrealists was also intended to be humorous. One of surrealism's main supports was the work of Freud, but the surrealists also drew inspiration from Lewis Carroll's *Alice in Wonderland,* the works of the French poet Arthur Rimbaud, and the writings of America's Edgar Allan Poe. Key figures in the movement, besides Breton, included the painters Max Ernst, Joan Miró, Yves Tanguy, Paul Klee, and René Magritte; the poet Paul Éluard; and the photographer Man Ray.

Having decided to become a surrealist, Dalí acted quickly. With the help of a few friends, he wrote a strongly worded attack on Catalan intellectuals. Printed on yellow paper and entitled *Manifest Groc* or *Yellow Manifesto,* the document excoriated the Catalans for not being modern enough. Also influenced by futurism, the manifesto proclaimed that automobile shows were more dynamic and alive than salons where landscape paintings were exhibited; boxing, jazz, the gramophone, and electric light were declared superior to art that was based on tradition. Dalí followed up with a public lecture in which he urged that folklore be abolished and that the old part of Barcelona be razed to the ground.

Dalí's outrageous behavior soon extended to his friend Lorca. When *Romancero gitano* (Gypsy Romance), a collection of Lorca's poetry, was published in 1928 to immediate and universal acclaim, Dalí wrote to the poet: "I've read your book calmly and I cannot refrain from making a few comments. Of course I can agree in no respect with the opinion of the big *putrefactos* [rotten] pigs who have commented on it. . . . Your poetry is tied hand and foot to old poetry. Perhaps you may consider certain images daring . . . but I can tell you your poetry is limited to illustration of the most stereotyped and conformist areas." Seven years would go by before Lorca would speak to Dalí again.

Meanwhile, in Paris, Luis Buñuel officially joined the surrealist movement in January 1929. As he had professional film experience by this time, he decided to explore the use of the medium as a surrealist vehicle. In need of a script, Buñuel visited Dalí in Figueres and asked if he was interested in working on a surrealist film. Not surprisingly, Dalí consented.

Buñuel and Dalí completed the script in only six days. The historic collaboration was described in a letter that Buñuel wrote shortly afterward: "We had to look for the plot line. Dalí said to me, 'I dreamed last night of ants swarming around in my hands,' and I said, 'Good Lord, and I dreamed that I had sliced somebody or other's eye. There's the film, let's go and make it.'"

Buñuel went on to describe how he and Dalí made a conscious decision to follow the implications they found in Freud: "We wrote with minds open to the first ideas that came into them and at the same time systematically rejecting everything that arose from our culture and education. They had to be images that would surprise us and that we would both accept without discussion. Nothing else."

The film certainly had no shortage of surprises. In addition to the sliced eyeball and the hand swarming with ants, the script called for many strange scenes. For example, two priests are seen lying on a floor, being dragged by ropes attached to a grand piano, on the top of which are two dead donkeys. The film was titled *Un chien andalou* (An Andalusian Dog), a phrase that members of the avant-garde Resi group had used to describe poets that they disliked. Because Lorca was from Andalusia, he felt the title of the film was a direct reference to him, and this increased his estrangement from his former friends.

Buñuel persuaded his mother to put up the money needed to make the film, and Dalí finally succeeded in convincing his father to give him the funds to go to Paris. Dalí arrived in the French capital in April 1929. He soon called on Joan Miró, who took him out to dinner. Miró planned to introduce Dalí to prominent members of society who were interested in the arts. Noticing that Dalí was very shy and did not have the appropriate clothes for high-society dinners, Miró tried to give Dalí a few pointers. Dalí merely replied, "I prefer to begin with rotten donkeys. This is the most urgent, the other things will come by themselves." Time would soon prove him right.

The shooting of *Un chien andalou* proved to be almost as surrealistic as the final 17-minute film. Dalí made the stuffed donkeys obtained for the film appear putrid by pouring huge containers of glue over them. The opening shot of a girl's eye being sliced by a razor was filmed in a slaughterhouse, using the eye of an ox; Buñuel was so affected by the filming of this scene that he became ill for several days. Dalí, heading for a

nervous breakdown himself, played one of the priests in the film. The film's leading man, Pierre Batcheff, was a drug addict, who showed up for work smelling of ether—he committed suicide on the final day of filming.

While in Paris, Dalí was introduced to a number of artists, prominent members of society, and intellectual figures such as Breton. Still, he did not find the immediate success that he had hoped for. He formed the habit of lugging around a painting with him wherever he went, in the hopes of getting a contract or arranging an exhibition. He talked to Camille

*In a scene from* Un chien andalou, *a man drags a pair of priests (the one on the right played by Dalí) and two grand pianos laden with dead donkeys. Dalí called the film "an animated painting" and proudly proclaimed that it broke "all cinematic rules."*

Goëmans, a Belgian art dealer, about a contract, but he could never get him to sign anything.

By the end of May, Dalí had managed to sell only one painting. Even worse, away from his family and old friends, he had no one to help him negotiate the practicalities of life. He was even terrified of using the Métro, Paris's subway system, by himself. And although Dalí could be a very entertaining and charming talker, he was extremely shy. He often wandered the streets, trying to meet women, but he usually ended up sitting on a bench in a park, weeping from sheer frustration and loneliness.

By this time, Dalí was thoroughly disheartened and decided to return to Spain. Even the scheduled showing of his film failed to excite him because he felt that the actors were poor and that the script was "full of poetic weaknesses." Even worse, in his eyes, was his failure to obtain a contract from Goëmans. He left for home, feeling that he had failed to make an impression. He had no idea that *Un chien andalou* was about to make him and Buñuel the talk of Paris.

# SCANDALOUS SUCCESS

When Dalí returned from Paris he painted a new work, *Dismal Sport,* which confirms that he had found a style that expressed his own vision. While this new style showed the influences of other painters, such as de Chirico and Max Ernst, the overall effect and vision were uniquely his own. Whereas *Honey Is Sweeter Than Blood* was an important transitional work, *Dismal Sport* demonstrates that Dalí had finally found himself as an artist.

Artistic triumphs aside, Dalí was showing signs of a deep disturbance. He was subject to fits of hysteria, during which time he would lie on the ground, laughing uncontrollably, for no apparent reason. One of his biographers, Meredith Etherington-Smith, interprets Dalí's behavior as showing a desperate need to break free from his father, on whom he was still financially dependent. His trip to Paris may also have made Dalí realize that he was poorly equipped to handle the practical side of life. If he had trouble with a simple matter such as using the subway, how could he possibly move to a foreign country and make a living there?

But Dalí had made more of an impression while he was in Paris than he probably realized. While there, he had met Paul Éluard, who had promised to visit Dalí in Spain. When Éluard came, he brought along

*Dalí strikes a casual pose as the SS* Normandie *enters New York harbor in December 1936. At this point in his career, Dalí was the best known of the surrealists—his new status brought fame, money, and controversy, all of which he greatly enjoyed.*

61

his wife, Gala. Other surrealists were in Cadaqués during the summer of 1929, and while they were impressed with Dalí, they were also disturbed by some of his talk and by one of the more explicit images in *Dismal Sport*. The painting went too far even by their standards, and Gala was deputed to speak to Dalí about this.

Dalí was very attracted to Gala, and she was sympathetic to even his strangest behavior. Though her husband returned to Paris, Gala spent the rest of the summer in Cadaqués. Dalí began to court her, and

The First Days of Spring, *painted in 1929, is one of the earliest works that show Dalí's fully matured style. Taking his cue from Sigmund Freud's psychological theories, Dalí tried to paint the contents of the subconscious mind.*

when she returned to Paris, she carried with her a suitcase full of Dalí's writings. She also brought *Dismal Sport* to Goëmans, who had finally signed a contract with Dalí for a one-man show at the end of November 1929.

Dalí worked hard to prepare for the show. Perhaps he sensed that he was on the verge of a decisive breakthrough. He had already heard of the excitement *Un chien andalou* was causing in Paris. When André Breton saw the film, he immediately acclaimed it, saying it was the first genuinely surrealist film. Picasso was one of many luminaries who attended a private showing in June. The vicomtesse de Noailles, an extremely cultivated patron of the arts, was so impressed that she arranged another private showing at her home. When the film had its public premiere, it was immediately controversial: dozens of articles were written about it, and the film's merits were examined at length from every conceivable angle. The talk of all Paris, the movie enjoyed a nine-month run.

The good luck that had eluded Dalí on his trip to Paris now seemed to come of its own accord when he returned. Not only did Dalí have a one-man show in Paris, but André Breton himself wrote the preface to the catalog. Breton was lavish in his praise, stating that "for the first time the windows of the mind had opened wide."

Dalí had Gala Éluard on his mind as much as his show. His first act upon arriving had been to buy her roses, although with typical confusion he had managed to botch even this simple transaction and ended up spending all the money he had with him on the flowers. By this time, the two were madly in love, and Gala managed to convince Dalí that they should take a kind of honeymoon. Amazingly, Dalí left with Gala for Sitges in Spain and was not even present for the opening of the show, the most important of his life. At the end of the month in Sitges, Dalí had become so identified with Gala that he referred to the Paris show as "our" exhibition.

It is difficult to determine exactly who Gala Éluard was, for she had resolved early on to remain a mysterious figure. A Russian by birth, she had met Paul Éluard in a sanatorium in Switzerland where they had both gone to recuperate from tuberculosis, an often fatal disease early in the century. They married and had a daughter, whom Gala essentially always ignored. Gala also had a constant need for new romantic attachments, and Éluard did not object to her having affairs with other men. When she became involved with Dalí, Eluard did not feel threatened, believing that this would be just another fling. He did not understand his wife's passion for money and luxury. Gala had already realized that a poet would never be able to keep her in comfort, but she eventually came to feel that Dalí might have the potential to earn lots of money. When she decided that she wanted something, she kept after it with steely determination.

When Dalí and Gala left Sitges, Dalí decided to visit his family, feeling guilty for having been out of touch for a month. Things started out badly, as Dalí's father asked how much money he had left from Goëmans's advance. Dalí, helpless with money, rummaged in his pockets and was only able to produce some torn French francs. The elder Dalí was also upset because of stories he had heard concerning Gala's reputation. Salvador's sister, Ana María, who would later blame Gala and the surrealists for corrupting her brother, joined in the fray. Just as things reached a climax, Buñuel arrived. He later recounted what he witnessed: "Suddenly the door flew open, and, purple with rage, Dalí's father threw his son out, calling him every name in the book."

*Continued on page 73*

# The Paintings of
# Salvador Dalí

*Portdogué and Mt. Pani from Ayuntamiento* (1926)

*The Basket of Bread* (1926)

*La Main (Les Remords de Conscience)* (1930)

*Shades of Night Descending* (1931)

*The Disintegration of the Persistence of Memory* (1952–54)

*Nature Morte Vivant (Still Life—Fast moving)* (1956)

*The Discovery of America by Christopher Columbus* (Also known
as *The Dream of Christopher Columbus*) (1958–59)

*The Hallucinogenic Toreador* (1969–70)

*Continued from page 64*

While Buñuel had arrived at a very bad time, he brought sensational news: following the wild success of *Un chien andalou,* the vicomtesse de Noailles's husband had given Buñuel one million francs to make a new film. Moreover, it was to be only the third picture ever made in France with sound. Naturally, Buñuel wanted Dalí to help. As if this were not enough, Buñuel informed Dalí that Goëmans had sold every painting in Dalí's exhibition at high prices.

Dalí and Buñuel immediately left for Cadaqués to work on the new film, which came to be called *L'age d'or* (The Golden Age). The film is a violent attack on established society and religion. Work on this film did not go smoothly, however, for Dalí and Buñuel had different ideas about what the film should be. Dalí felt that Buñuel was making the film into a simple attack on the church, whereas Dalí wanted both humor and "mythic vision." After disagreeing for two weeks, Buñuel left Dalí to complete the film on his own.

After Buñuel left, Dalí received a letter from his father, who declared that he was disowning his son forever. His father had read about Salvador's lithograph of a heart, across which the artist had written that he sometimes spat on a picture of his mother. This was the last straw for the elder Salvador. Dalí would later explain that the inscription was only written for "psychoanalytical" reasons. Psychologists have noted that people often have unwanted thoughts of attacking or insulting people that they love and are close to, and Dalí, in keeping with surrealist theory, apparently was trying to confront such thoughts. It is also possible that Dalí really wanted a final break with his father and was trying to provoke his father into denouncing him. Whatever the truth of the matter, the letter from his father devastated Dalí. The artist shaved off all his

*Dalí met Gala Éluard, wife of surrealist poet Paul Éluard, in 1929. Dalí later wrote, "Without love, without Gala, I would no longer be Dalí. That is a truth I will never stop shouting or living. She is my blood, my oxygen."*

hair, buried it on the beach, and returned to Paris and Gala.

When they were reunited, Gala and Dalí departed for the French Riviera, where they spent another "honeymoon." There they received a letter from the vicomte de Noailles, warning them that Goëmans was going bankrupt. Gala and Dalí were running out of money and put their heads together to figure out a method of surviving. They hit upon the device of asking the vicomte to commission a major painting but to pay for it in advance. Gala, playing a role that she would repeat numberless times, then offered some business advice: Dalí should ask for a very large sum for the painting, 29,000 francs. He agreed, and Gala left for Paris with the proposal, which the vicomte accepted.

While Dalí had been vacationing on the Riviera, he came to realize that he needed to be near Cadaqués in order to be happy and to derive inspiration for his painting. When he and Gala tried to settle in Cadaqués, they found that no one would help them. Dalí's father had informed the town's inhabitants in no uncertain terms that his son was an outcast.

Dalí took the money from his commission and used it to buy a shack that Lidia Nogueres owned in nearby Port Lligat. He and Gala now lived in almost pioneer style. He painted all day, while Gala critiqued his work, transcribed his nearly illegible notes, and constantly encouraged him. Now their only friends in the Empordà were Lidia Nogueres, who remained loyal to Dalí, and a few local fishermen.

For several years, Dalí and Gala lived a rather strange existence, shuttling between Paris and Port Lligat. It was an endless round of grueling work, alternating with forays into Paris society that were designed to make Dalí as famous and successful as possible. At times, Gala and Dalí would be flush with money, and at other times, they would not have enough to buy food and clothes. Some days, they would be in the most prestigious homes in Paris; on other days, they would be back in Port Lligat, where their only neighbor was a defrocked priest and the only people who would speak to them were fishermen even poorer than Gala and Dalí.

Part of the reason for their poverty was *L'age d'or*. Soon after the film opened, right-wing fanatics dis-

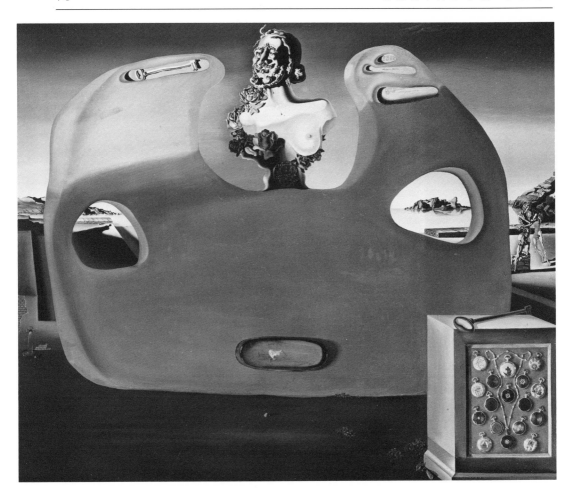

rupted a showing by firing guns in the theater, throwing ink on the screen, setting off stink bombs, smashing glass, and destroying seats. They then went into the lobby where paintings by Dalí, Tanguy, Ernst, and Miró were on display and destroyed them. The Paris police—who, incidentally, had been one of the film's main targets—did not feel any need to protect artistic freedom. The prefect of police wrote an open letter attacking the film and calling its makers "scum." The influential newspaper *Le Figaro* suggested that the police suppress surrealism. Indeed, the film caused such a scandal that the vicomte de Noailles's mother

*Dalí's 1932 painting* Memory of the Child-Woman. *The coasts of Port Lligat and Cadaqués are represented in the painting's background: Dalí scholars Eleanor and Reynolds Morse have suggested that this reflects the feud between Dalí and his father that was going on at the time.*

had to intercede with the Vatican to keep her son from being excommunicated from the Catholic church. Not surprisingly, much of Paris society was afraid for some time to buy Dalí's works.

Things finally cooled off, and Dalí was more in demand than ever. During these years in the early 1930s, he painted some of his greatest works. He enjoyed working hard and relaxed by eating seafood and frequenting the beaches of his beloved Empordà.

One evening in 1931, Dalí had a particularly rare inspiration. He had been painting a landscape near Port Lligat and had quit for the evening. Gala had gone out, and Dalí had a headache. After enjoying some Camembert cheese, he sat at the dinner table, contemplating the soft cheese and thinking about the general concept of softness. Then he went to inspect the canvas that he was currently working on, just as he did every evening before retiring. Suddenly, he "saw" two limp watches, soft as Camembert cheese. He immediately set to work, and when Gala returned, he showed her the picture with the watches. He asked her if she thought she would still remember the painting in three years. Gala replied that no one who saw the painting would ever forget it. She was right—that evening Dalí had painted *The Persistence of Memory,* one of the 20th century's most famous works of art.

One of the tasks that Gala had assumed was getting Dalí's writings published. At the end of 1930, Dalí's first book, *The Visible Woman,* appeared. In it, Dalí discussed one of his major theories, something he called the "paranoiac-critical" method. The theory was inspired by Dalí's childhood memories of the rocks of Cadaqués, which seemed to be other objects at the same time that they were rocks. The method was called "paranoiac" because, just as a paranoid person imagines things that are not real, so, too, the aim of the exercise is to see other objects within a single object. Dalí urges the artist to simulate a deranged mental state without becoming deranged.

The theory is generally credited as being Dalí's greatest contribution to surrealism. Breton wrote, "Dalí has endowed Surrealism with an instrument of primary importance, specifically the paranoiac-critical method." Dalí put the theory into practice by painting the outline of the first image that came to him in a dream or fantasy; then he filled in the space with other images that the first image suggested. This technique gave the surrealists a practical tool for reaching the depths of the human mind.

In the 1930s, Dalí's energies were fully unleashed. Picasso once remarked that Dalí's mind raced like an "outboard motor" that ran nonstop. Always creating, Dalí painted, drew, traveled, wrote, lectured, and theorized. His spectacular appearances at lectures and parties became a kind of "performance art." He garnered headlines that made his name almost synonymous in the public mind with the surrealist movement itself. One of his more colorful performances was a lecture in which he entered the hall led by two Russian wolfhounds on leashes and wearing a diving suit, a jeweled dagger stuck under his belt. Unfortunately, the diving suit's helmet had been too securely tightened, and Dalí almost suffocated before workers succeeded in removing it.

The surrealists met regularly to discuss the state of their movement. Breton presided at these meetings in an almost dictatorial manner, wearing a green suit and smoking a green pipe. At one of these meetings, Dalí and fellow surrealist André Thirion were assigned the task of finding a means of drawing the group closer together. Thirion suggested a campaign against the church, but Dalí showed real creativity by conceiving of the "surrealist object." In a 1931 article, he defined

*A still from Dalí and Buñuel's* L'age d'or *shows skeletons wearing the ecclesiastical garb of the Catholic church. The film's controversial nature hurt Dalí's career for a while, and he wrote of the final version, "It was but a caricature of my ideas."*

surrealist objects as those "objects which lend themselves to the minimum of mechanical functions [and] are based on phantasms and representations capable of being aroused by the accomplishments of unconscious acts." One of Dalí's better-known surrealist objects was the "Aphrodisiac Jacket," an ordinary man's coat to which many small shot glasses had been attached.

In 1933, Dalí decided to attempt a reconciliation with his father. Although his father at first ordered him out of the house, Dalí begged for forgiveness, and the elder man gave in. The reunion between father and son was very brief, however. That same day, Catalonia was plunged into chaos as Catalan separatists declared their independence from Spain. Dalí and

Gala were awakened in the middle of the night by the sounds of gunfire, and they barely made it out of Spain alive.

The following year, Dalí created a crisis within the surrealist movement when he began to talk admiringly of Adolf Hitler, whose right-wing Nazi party was gaining strength in Germany. Breton wrote to Dalí, demanding an explanation. Dalí responded that he was not a "Hitlerian," but he refused "to interpret Hitlerism in the manner in which it is explained by the Communists." (The Communists and other left-wing parties were the first to recognize the danger posed by Hitler and his followers, who eventually

*The 1940 painting* Old Age, Adolescence and Infancy *is an example of Dalí's paranoiac-critical method, in which an object can be seen as two different things. The two large holes in the wall of the house can also be seen as the outlines of faces, for example. Art historians have traced the technique to the 15th-century Italian master Leonardo da Vinci.*

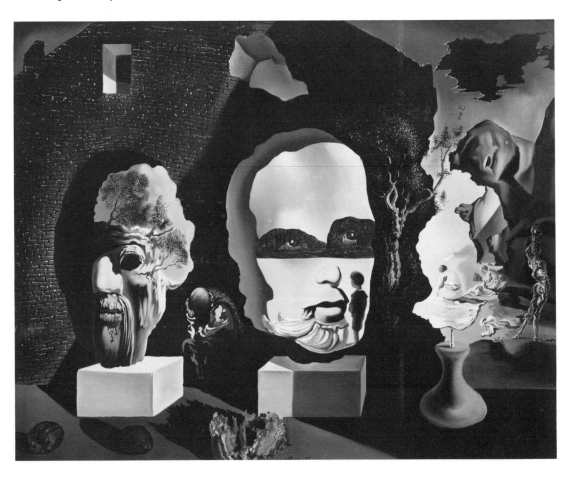

plunged the world into war as well as murdering millions of innocent people—but the Communists also showed that they could be just as brutal and intolerant as the Nazis.) Dalí refused to accept any restrictions on what he could say or paint. To him, everything seemed fair game for surrealist creativity; he pointed out that he had often painted images of Vladimir Lenin, the hero of the Communists.

However, when Dalí painted Hitler, the surrealists saw it as a glorification of the Nazi leader, and Dalí was summoned to what amounted to a trial. Dalí came to the meeting with a high fever, wearing seven sweaters and holding a thermometer in his mouth. He explained that he had painted both Hitler and Lenin as they had appeared to him in dreams, being faithful to the surrealist principle of exploring the unconscious. He went on to say, "All taboos are forbidden, or else a list has to be made of those to be observed, and let Breton formally state that the kingdom of Surrealist poetry is nothing but a little domain used for the house arrest of those convicted felons placed under surveillance by the vice squad or the Communist party."

At the end of the meeting, Dalí swore that he was not an enemy of the working class, and the incident blew over. Shortly thereafter, Dalí wrote a letter to a friend, saying that he was having second thoughts about his humorous attitude toward dictators. Still, the "trial" was a harbinger of future tension between Dalí and the surrealists, led by their "pope," André Breton.

# INDEPENDENCE
# OF THE
# IMAGINATION

*Salvador and Gala Dalí at a ball they gave in 1941 in Pebble Beach, California. Called "Night in a Surrealist Forest," the event was a spectacular success, attended by celebrities such as the movie stars Ginger Rogers and Clark Gable.*

Around 1931, Alfred Barr, the director of New York's Museum of Modern Art, had met Dalí and been quite taken with him, describing him as "a veritable radar of modern art." He had told Dalí, "Come to the States. You'll be a lightning success." Around the same time, a young art dealer from New York, Julien Levy, bought *The Persistence of Memory* for $250. In 1933, Levy organized Dalí's first one-man New York show, and the favorable reviews seemed to bear out Barr's earlier statement. Dalí wrote that the American reviews showed "a comprehension a hundred times more objective and better informed . . . than most of the commentaries on my work that had appeared in Europe."

Dalí decided to go to the United States and see for himself how he would be received. First, however, he and Gala married at the urging of Paul Éluard. Éluard had come to realize that Dalí was more than a passing fancy for Gala, and he was willing to let her go. In 1934, Dalí borrowed $500 from Picasso to make the trip to New York, and the American press fell in love with his eccentricities from the very beginning. Levy had organized another show at which Dalí, unable to speak English, read a surrealist manifesto that he had

83

written out phonetically: "Surrealism is irresistible and terrifyingly contagious. Beware! I bring you Surrealism. Already many people in New York have been infected by the lifegiving and marvelous source of Surrealism."

Indeed, it did seem that the contagion was spreading. At the end of Dalí's visit, a Dream Ball was given for Dalí by his prominent American hostess, Caresse Crosby. Those invited, most of them members of high society, were told to come dressed as their dreams. The guests were greeted by a doorman seated in a rocking chair, and they exchanged their invitation cards for a link of sausage. Among the many effects Dalí had organized were a bathtub that appeared to be sliding down a flight of stairs and the figure of a cow wearing a white wedding veil.

By this time, Dalí and Gala's repeated attempts to be accepted in high society had succeeded splendidly. One young society member who would play an important role in Dalí's life was Edward James, an English art collector who, inheriting a fortune at the age of 21, had immediately spent large sums on surrealist art. Besides having a great passion for surrealism, James saw himself as a kind of participant in the movement. He suggested surrealist schemes to Dalí, such as a dinner party at which dwarfs would stand on the table holding candelabra; the guests, James suggested, would be served fish skins stuffed with steak. Dalí and James soon became inseparable.

Meanwhile, Dalí's old friend Lorca had achieved equal fame, as Lorca's plays and poetry were widely admired. Although there is no record of their having written to each other before 1934, the two men undoubtedly kept up with each other's careers through mutual friends. Dalí wrote to Lorca in 1934 and suggested that they collaborate on an opera that Dalí was planning. Although there is no record of

Lorca's response to the proposal, the two men finally met the following year when Dalí, Gala, and James visited Barcelona.

The reunion was a happy one. Lorca was thrilled to see Dalí again and did not try to hide his pleasure. Lorca told a journalist friend, "We are twin spirits. Here's the proof: seven years without seeing each other and yet we agree on everything as if we'd never stopped talking since then. Salvador Dalí is a genius, a genius." Indeed, they talked so long that Lorca caused a scandal that evening by failing to show up at a concert that had been especially organized in his honor. Instead, he spent the evening at the café across from the Ritz, where he and Dalí had enjoyed so many happy hours in the past. A witness noticed that Dalí wore a tie made out of newspaper and that James wore a kilt, apparently to amaze the Spaniards.

Lorca and Dalí met at the café several days in a row. Dalí urged Lorca to accompany them to Italy, where they were going to stay at one of James's many international homes. Lorca declined. It was the last time that the two men would ever see each other. In 1936, in the midst of the Spanish Civil War, the poet was murdered by right-wingers who objected to his left-wing sympathies and his homosexuality. Dalí would long blame himself for Lorca's death, thinking that if he had been able to convince Lorca to come to Italy, his friend would have survived.

In 1936, Dalí branched out into interior decoration by undertaking to redecorate James's Italian hunting lodge. Among the changes Dalí made were placing sculpted blankets over the chimney tops, hanging plaster bed sheets from the windows, and installing a huge clock in the chimney—made of hand-painted glass, the clock showed the day of the week rather than the hour of the day. During the remodeling, Dalí complained to one of the architects with whom he was working, "It's very difficult to shock the world every 24 hours."

James was alive to any idea that Dalí proposed. Among them was the *Lobster Telephone,* perhaps Dalí's most famous surrealist object. Dalí fashioned a lobster from plaster of paris and attached it to a clip, and every telephone in James's London residence soon had a lobster sitting on top of it.

On July 18, 1936, the Spanish Civil War began when right-wing forces led by General Francisco Franco rebelled against Spain's Second Republic. Dalí's reactions to the war did not do him credit. At first, when the left seemed to be winning, he cheered the Communists and anarchists; then, when it appeared that the right would win, he began to praise Franco, who eventually became Spain's dictator. The

Lobster Telephone, *one of Dalí's most famous surrealist objects. Dalí had invented the concept of the surrealist object in 1931.*

best that can be said for Dalí is that he placed his art before everything. Feeling that he could only really paint in his homeland, he feared that if he backed the losing side in the war he could never return to Spain after the shooting stopped. Thus, while Picasso painted *Guernica* to protest fascism and refused to return to Spain as long as Franco remained in power, Dalí would not even donate any artwork to raise funds for Spanish Republican refugees. While his support of Franco did make it possible for him to return to Spain after the war, it also complicated the rest of his life.

By the late 1930s, Gala Dalí had become her husband's business manager as well as his secretary, cook, and main critic. She pushed Dalí to paint more and more, and she especially encouraged him to do commissioned works because they could command fat fees. Once she had only rubbed elbows with famous fashion designers, such as Coco Chanel and Elsa Schiaparelli; now she wore their clothing and was not happy with anything less stylish and expensive. Dalí began to feel that, because of the unrelenting pressure Gala put on him to make money, he could not do the kind of paintings he wanted. He turned to Edward James for help. James came to his rescue by offering to support the Dalís for three years in return for ownership of all the works Dalí painted between 1936 and 1939.

James made this offer partly because of his enthusiasm for art, and partly because he and Dalí had become lovers. Their relationship would last until the beginning of World War II in 1939. Few details of the affair are known, but Gala was aware of it and generally accepted it. When she occasionally made a scene out of jealousy, James was always able to calm her down by giving her expensive dresses or jewelry.

Jealousy from other quarters complicated Dalí's artistic life after New York's Museum of Modern Art

*A Spanish woman sits with her few possessions outside a bombed-out block of houses at the end of the Spanish Civil War in 1939. During the three-year course of the war, Dalí switched his allegiance from the Communists and anarchists to the Fascists, who were eventually victorious.*

mounted a major show on surrealism. When the show opened, *Time* magazine put Dalí's face on its cover, photographed by Man Ray. *Time* wrote, "Surrealism would never have attracted its present attention in the U.S. were it not for a handsome 32-year-old Catalan with a soft voice and a clipped cinemator's moustache, Salvador Dalí." Other surrealists were understandably envious and therefore attacked Dalí. Breton was especially upset, feeling that his status as leader of the surrealists was now endangered by the publicity Dalí had gained.

In 1937, the Dalís traveled to California to meet the stars of Hollywood. Dalí had long admired the Marx Brothers, proclaiming them to be true surrealists. He especially liked Harpo, and the two men hit it off while Dalí was in Hollywood. Dalí even wrote a script for a film to be made with Harpo Marx as the star. The script was called *Giraffes on Horseback Salad;* unfortunately, it was never made into a film.

Freed from Gala's demands for money by James's patronage, Dalí was able to paint some of the major works of his career during the late 1930s. One of the most important, *The Metamorphosis of Narcissus,* is an example of his paranoiac-critical method and is based on the Greek myth about the beautiful youth who falls in love with his own reflection in a lake. In the painting—in fact, a self-portrait—Narcissus turns into a limestone hand that holds an egg out of which a narcissus flower blooms. One of Dalí's biographers, Meryle Secrest, interprets the painting's theme of reflection as a comment on Dalí's "endless self-absorption": "Dalí, who had constructed a grandiose self to compensate for the freak he secretly believed himself to be, was expressing some deep truths about his state of mind."

There is no doubt that Dalí saw the painting as one of his major works, for he wrote a poem to accompany it. In the poem he quotes two Port Lligat fishermen (probably Lidia Nogueres's sons). One asks, "What's wrong with that chap, glaring at himself all day long in his looking glass?" The other replies, "If you really want to know, he has a bulb in his head." Dalí explained that this Catalan expression meant a mental illness or complex. "In other words," explains Secrest, "not only had Dalí become two distinctly different people—he was perfectly aware of the inner fragmentation." It was a fragmentation that would eventually cost him dearly.

Friction between Dalí and the surrealist movement became more frequent as the years went by. Finally, the surrealists expelled Dalí from the movement, probably more for reasons of jealousy than anything else. Breton could not bear to see Dalí reap all the fame and publicity that so easily came his way. Dalí, for his part, had never hidden his ambition to take Breton's position as the supreme head of the movement. In fairness to Breton, who had a strong distaste for what he considered "perversions," he had from the first felt that Dalí ran the risk of misunderstanding or misapplying surrealist doctrine. In his introduction to the catalog for Dalí's first one-man show in Paris, Breton had said that Dalí was at a kind of crossroads: he could choose either talent or genius, vice or virtue. In the catalog, Breton had betrayed some discomfort with what he felt to be Dalí's misuse of psychological texts for deliberate sensationalism.

The art historian Dawn Ades points out that Dalí had always been indifferent to the surrealists' political and social agenda. When he was expelled from the movement, Dalí expressed his point of view in his typically witty way: "The only difference between the Surrealists and me is that I am a Surrealist."

Once they threw him out, the surrealists realized that they needed Dalí to keep their movement alive and in the public eye. As far as much of the public was concerned, Dalí was correct: if he was not a surrealist, who was? Thus, when the International Surrealist Exhibition was conceived in 1938, the organizers tried to make use of Dalí's fame by naming him a "special adviser" to the exhibition. Dalí was not invited to submit any paintings, however. But he had his revenge when one of his creations—a taxi filled with greenery and live snails—became the exhibition's main attraction.

Dalí enjoyed an even greater pleasure later in the year when he met Sigmund Freud, whose theories had exerted such a powerful influence on Dalí's work. Having read in the newspaper that the Nazis had

*Surrealist Poster (1934) has been seen as a forerunner of the pop art that became the rage during the 1960s. Dalí often referred to his work as "painted photographs," and his realism has gone against the predominant tendency in 20th century art—abstraction.*

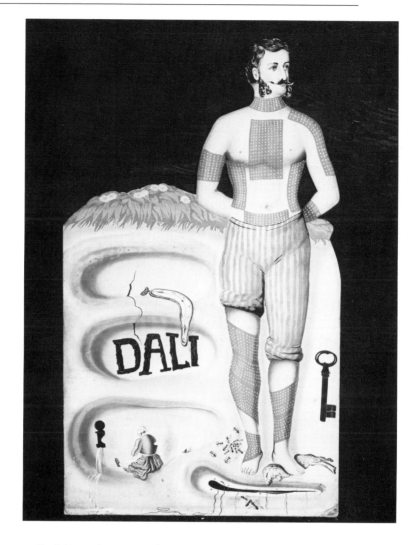

exiled Freud to London, Dalí set in motion a campaign to get an audience with the great man. Accompanied by Edward James, he called on Freud during the summer. He had brought along a sketchbook and made several drawings of Freud. While Dalí sketched, Freud remarked, "That boy looks like a fanatic. Small wonder they have civil war in Spain if they look like that." When Dalí and Freud talked, Freud observed that in the works of other artists he searched for the subconscious, but in Dalí's works he looked for the

conscious mind. Freud must have been impressed, for
the following day he wrote to Dalí's friend who had
arranged the meeting, saying, "I have to thank you
indeed for the introduction of our visitor of yesterday.
Until now I was inclined to regard the Surrealists—
who seem to have adopted me as their patron saint—
as 100 percent fools. . . . This young Spaniard . . . has
suggested to me a different estimate."

In 1939, the Dalís made another trip to New York,
where Julien Levy was organizing a new Dalí exhibition. By this time, Dalí had branched out into the
fashion world by joining forces with Schiaparelli and
creating window displays for the designer's Paris store.
It is not surprising, therefore, that when Dalí was in
New York, the Bonwit Teller department store proposed that he decorate some of their windows. When
he saw the store's extensive workshops for creating
displays, Dalí became so excited that he almost forgot
to specify his pay. Given two windows to decorate,
Dalí decided to use the themes of day and night and
worked on the very intricate displays all night with
Gala's help. When he returned to inspect the results
the following day, he was absolutely livid to find that
they had been altered in response to some complaints
from the public. Dalí went inside and demanded that
the windows either be restored to the way he had
created them or that his name be removed. Bonwit
Teller refused.

Dalí then went into the "Day" window, which
contained a bathtub filled with water. He tried to turn
the tub over, but it slipped and crashed into the huge
plate-glass window, sending thousands of glass splin-
ters flying onto Fifth Avenue. Luckily, no one was
injured.

Dalí calmly jumped out of the window, but a
detective who had happened to be passing on a bus
had seen him break the window and arrested him.

Appearing before a judge in night court, Dalí was given a suspended sentence and released, but he was ordered to pay for the window. The judge held that Dalí's action may have been excessive, but that all artists have the right to defend the integrity of their work. The incident made Dalí both instantly famous and a popular hero. When his show opened at Levy's gallery, long lines formed in the street, and people fought to get inside. Two weeks later, *Life* magazine reported that Dalí, at the age of 34, had become one of the world's richest young artists.

Controversy seemed to follow Dalí wherever he went. He had signed a contract to create an exhibition for the 1939 World's Fair, which was held in Queens, New York. Called "The Dream of Venus," it was Dalí's attempt to depict a dream that Venus, the goddess of love, had about her birthplace. James, who had formed a corporation to help make the exhibit, worked intimately with Dalí on the project. Things did not go smoothly at all, primarily because of the intrusion of various investors. As part of the presentation, Dalí planned to recreate *The Birth of Venus,* a renowned painting by Sandro Botticelli, but Dalí intended to substitute the head of a fish for that of Venus. One investor found this to be too outlandish and persuaded the World's Fair officials to ban it.

Dalí responded with a parody of the U.S. Declaration of Independence, entitled "Declaration of the Independence of the Imagination and of the Rights of Man to his Own Madness." He wrote, "The committee ... has forbidden me to erect on the exterior of 'The Dream of Venus': the image of a woman with the head of a fish. These are their exact words: 'A woman with a tail of a fish is possible; a woman with the head of a fish is impossible.'" Dalí went on to point out that if such committees had existed in ancient Greece, the Greeks would never have created their rich mythology. "Any authentically original idea," he continued, "is systematically rejected, toned down, mauled . . . and even worse—reduced to the most monstrous of mediocrities. The excuse is always the vulgarity of the vast majority of the public. I insist that this is absolutely false. The public is infinitely superior to the rubbish that is fed to it daily."

Unfortunately, the affair led to a distancing between Dalí and James, for Dalí had returned to France when the difficulties began, and James felt that Dalí had left him holding the bag. The romance between the two men would eventually come to an end, primarily because Gala Dalí felt threatened by it. She

*The 1940 painting* Daddy Longlegs of the Evening . . . Hope! *shows Dalí's preoccupation with World War II, which had just broken out in Europe. The title of the painting is derived from a French legend that seeing a daddy longlegs in the evening brings good luck.*

could tolerate an affair, but not a relationship in which there was a chance that someone else might become as important to Dalí as she was.

Upon his return to Europe, Dalí found the continent simmering on the brink of war. Gala was Jewish, and she would be in mortal danger if German troops were to occupy France—the Nazis had already begun their campaign of terror against the European Jews. At first the Dalís went to a town near the Spanish border so that they could easily slip into Spain in case German troops came near. Dalí—who consistently maintained that he had more talent as a writer than as a painter—worked for a while on an autobiographical volume, eventually entitled *The Secret Life of Salvador Dalí*.

When the Dalís finally left France, they passed through war-ravaged Catalonia, the sight of which reminded the artist of Francisco de Goya's drawings of Spain after it had been ravaged by French troops early in the 19th century. Reunited with his family, Dalí found that they had been far removed from his life of luxury and fame. His sister had been tortured and raped, and the dining-room floor was scorched by the fires that the anarchists had built to cook their food during the time they had occupied the Dalís' residence. He found no better at Port Lligat: his house had been ransacked, and all of its contents had disappeared. Many of the local fishermen who had been Dalí's friends had been killed.

Mindful of Lorca's fate in Spain and fearing the Nazis in France, Dalí and Gala seemed to have only one intelligent choice left: America. Caresse Crosby offered to let them stay with her, and Dalí telegraphed Edward James for money. James came through, as always, and in August 1939, the Dalís sailed to the United States.

# CLASSICAL NUCLEAR ART

The Dalís stayed at Caresse Crosby's house in the Virginia countryside for approximately one year, while Salvador painted, staged surrealist events, and continued to write his autobiography. Soon, however, the Dalís sought to recreate in America a pattern of life similar to the one they had become used to in Europe, where they had shuttled back and forth between Paris and Port Lligat. The closest approximations they could find in America were New York and Pebble Beach, California. In New York there were art galleries, wealthy patrons to cultivate, and good restaurants; in Pebble Beach, Dalí could be near the sea and enjoy the quiet he needed for painting.

Dalí may have found a congenial place to paint, but his contract with Edward James had come to an end. Once again, Gala began pressuring him to undertake commissioned works rather than the purely creative paintings he wanted to do. Most of the commissions he took during the 1940s were portraits of wealthy society women, such as Helena Rubenstein and Lady Mountbatten.

When Dalí had the time to paint what he liked, his work showed that he was taking a new direction. He had announced this in the invitations to his 1941 exhibition: "Salvador Dalí requests the pleasure of your company at his last scandal, the beginning of his

*Dalí paints a picture at the Walt Disney Studio for use in a film Disney never completed,* Destino. *Although Dalí long courted Hollywood, the only successful commercial film project he ever worked on was Alfred Hitchcock's* Spellbound.

classical painting." Dalí had made several trips to Italy in the 1930s, and while there he had studied Renaissance art extremely carefully, traveling out of his way to examine even the obscure works of important artists. The influence of this study now began to make itself felt, in works that Dalí described as having "more design, balance, and precise technique." Also on display at the exhibition were several pieces of jewelry and a crystal cup that he had designed.

Ever creative, Dalí also branched out into ballet. A Spanish patron Dalí had known in Europe, the marqués de Cuevas, had subsidized a ballet, *Bacchanale,* for which Dalí had designed the sets and costumes before embarking for America. When the war began, Cuevas had shipped the entire dance company, the famous Ballets Russes de Monte Carlo, across the Atlantic. *Bacchanale* had proven surprisingly popular, and Cuevas was now willing to sponsor a new ballet. He asked Dalí to write the libretto, in addition to designing scenery and costumes. This ballet, *Labyrinth,* was well received at New York's Metropolitan Opera House and then went on tour.

In 1942, Dalí's autobiography, *The Secret Life of Salvador Dalí,* was published. As autobiography, the book has to be taken with more than a grain of salt because the author took the same liberties with everyday reality as he did in his paintings. In writing *The Secret Life,* Dalí had little concern for literal truth. His purpose was more to give his own interpretations to the events of his life, to construct his own tongue-in-cheek mythology, a word picture of himself as a larger-than-life genius and artist.

Just as some of Dalí's pictures and films had shocked, so did his autobiography. The *New Yorker* magazine called it a "grinning nightmare of a book." The reviewer for the *New York Times* was particularly irritated by Dalí's "frank admission . . . that . . . he determined to capitalize on the stupidity of people and, in effect, make them pay for his living."

In 1945, Dalí's dream of a collaboration with Hollywood finally came true. The renowned British director Alfred Hitchcock had decided to make a film in which the psychoanalysis of an amnesia victim reveals clues to his identity and unravels the mystery about a murder that he believes he has committed. The film, *Spellbound,* starred Gregory Peck and Ingrid Bergman. It included an analysis of the protagonist's dreams, and Hitchcock requested that Dalí create the visual elements of the dream sequences. Dalí was enthusiastic about working with Hitchcock and created five black–and–white paintings for the film. When it was released, *Spellbound* received an Academy Award nomination for best picture.

An event of cataclysmic proportions that same year seized Dalí's imagination when the United States, seeking to force the surrender of Japan in the Pacific theater of World War II, dropped an atomic bomb on the Japanese city of Hiroshima. "The atomic explosion . . . shook me seismically," Dalí wrote. "Thenceforth, the atom was my favorite food for thought." Indeed, Dalí had long had a great interest in science, and when he became proficient in English he kept on top of the latest scientific developments with a subscription to *Scientific American* magazine. The distinctive atomic mushroom cloud that so haunted the world's imagination after Hiroshima began to show up in Dalí's canvases.

At the same time that Dalí was beginning to explore the atom, he also began to paint pictures with a religious theme. Interestingly, two canvases that Dalí painted at about the same time both used the image of the Madonna to explore Dalí's two new interests. The first, the *Madonna of Port Lligat,* completed in 1949, used Gala as a model for Jesus' mother. The second, *Exploding Raphaelesque Head,* was based on a painting of the Madonna by the 16th-century Italian artist Raphael. Dalí explained that "to the continuous waves of Raphael, I added discontinuous corpuscles to represent the world of today." Thus, in the latter painting, Dalí managed to combine his interest in classical painting, religious painting, and nuclear physics.

In 1948, Dalí returned to Spain for the first time since he had left it on the eve of World War II. He visited his family, although the emotional situation at home was still quite fragile. Everything fell apart in 1949 when Ana María Dalí published a book about her brother's early life. Reynolds Morse, a close friend of Dalí's, recalls being summoned to see Dalí when his sister's book came out: "Dalí was wound up and said, 'My sister has destroyed my image. I have worked all these years to prove what a monster I was and she has ruined my legend, she has proved I am just a nice little boy.'"

According to Ana María's biography, the Dalís were a happy family, and Salvador was a talented, decent young man who was corrupted by the surrealists. This account was given more credibility by Dalí's father's foreword to the book, in which he endorsed his daughter's account. The book definitively ended Dalí's relationship with both his father and his sister. Dalí never spoke to his father again, although he did attend his funeral in 1950.

Not surprisingly, the many changes in Dalí's art and philosophy since he had fled Europe for America created controversy within the art world. Edward James wrote Dalí a lengthy letter in which he laid out his concerns: "Your pretence at Catholicism is in the eyes of everybody a mere mockery. . . . You have told me time and time again that this would be your next step since you felt that the Papacy would be the eventual winner in Europe . . . after the various world

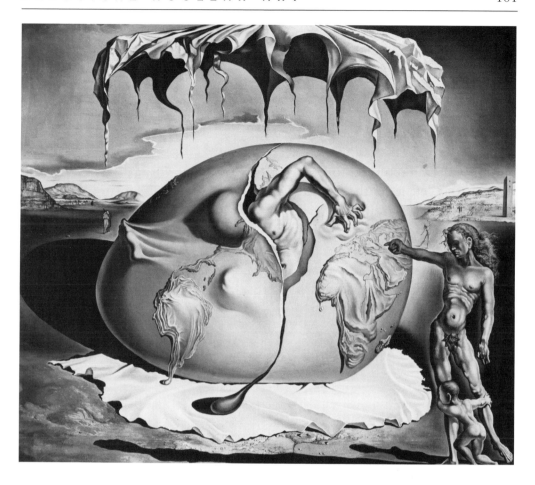

The 1943 painting Geopoliticus Child Watching the Birth of the New Man *is an example of the classical phase of Dalí's art. Dalí's interest in classicism resulted from the trips he made to Italy in the 1930s to study Renaissance art.*

conflicts of Communism and Fascism and Democracy had worn themselves out." In other words, James was accusing Dalí of doing the same thing that he had done during the Spanish Civil War— trying to get on the winning side instead of acting out of principle.

While some critics admired Dalí's religious art, many did not. One wrote that the art had "just about as much religious feeling as 'Through the night of doubt and sorrow' played on a Wurlitzer in the interval of a leg show." Still, Dalí's *Christ of Saint John of the Cross* has remained the best-selling postcard at the Glasgow Art Gallery in Scotland for 30 years, proving at least that much of the public was convinced of the artist's sincerity.

André Breton had also come to the United States during World War II, but his surrealist pronouncements, published in French, were generally ignored. Always jealous, Breton must therefore have been stung all the more by Dalí's ever-increasing fame. In 1942, Breton made an anagram from Dalí's name, transposing the letters to read "Avida Dollars"—avid (greedy) for dollars. Breton raged against Dalí for having sold out: "The rustle of paper money . . . has led the squeaking patent-leather shoes . . . into that soft-lit

*Dalí's 1960* The Ecumenical Council *demonstrates the artist's interest in religious themes, which began to appear in his work in 1949. Dalí painted this huge canvas to demonstrate his enthusiasm for Pope John XXIII's efforts to update the Catholic church.*

territory of Neo-Romanticism and the Waldorf-Astoria." Dalí replied by embracing the anagram, saying that it proved that he had good luck.

As part of Dalí's interest in science and math, he had become obsessed with rhinoceros horns, sunflowers, and cauliflowers as examples of "logarithmic perfection." In 1955, when Dalí gave a lecture at France's leading university, the Sorbonne, he arrived in a white Rolls-Royce filled with cauliflower. He opened his lecture with characteristic flamboyance: "Salvador Dalí has decided to make the most delirious announcement of his life in Paris, because . . . France is the most rational country in the world; on the contrary, I . . . come from Spain, which is the most irrational country in the world. . . . It is for this reason that it is good and necessary that from time to time Spaniards like Picasso and myself come to Paris to dazzle you."

To much applause, Dalí went on to explain his "delirious" theories about the rhinoceros horn and how it related to the work of the 17th-century Dutch artist Jan Vermeer, among other phenomena. With a slide of a rhinoceros's rear end projected on a screen, he brought down the house by saying, "I have analyzed this part of the rhinoceros with the result that it exactly resembles a layered sunflower. Therefore, the rhinoceros is not satisfied with carrying one of the most beautiful logarithmic curves on the end of his nose, but, besides, on his rear end he has a kind of galaxy of logarithmic curves in the form of a sunflower."

The audience was royally entertained, and the afternoon was a high-water mark for Dalí. Years after the surrealists had expelled him from their ranks, the public confirmed that, as far as they were concerned, Dalí was still the ultimate surrealist.

# "AVIDA DOLLARS"

In 1956, the year following Dalí's Sorbonne lecture, Joseph Forêt, an art publisher, visited Dalí in Port Lligat. Forêt lugged heavy lithographic stones with him in the hope that he could persuade Dalí to illustrate the most famous piece of Spanish literature, Miguel de Cervantes' *Don Quixote*. Dalí was not interested in the project, but when Forêt persisted, Dalí suggested that he might illustrate the book by filling bullets with ink and shooting them at the stones with a harquebus, an ancient firearm. Forêt agreed, and Dalí executed the lithographs as proposed, dubbing the results "Bulletism." When the lithographs fetched very high prices, it was enough to give even Dalí pause, for he realized that people would pay handsomely for almost anything signed with his name.

*A natural exhibitionist and a tireless seeker of publicity, Dalí mugs for a group of Girl Scouts. Because the artist was eager to explore regions of the mind society would prefer not to face, it is easy to forget that his works often have a playful dimension.*

Dalí would later say, "Whatever happens, my audience mustn't know whether I'm spoofing or being serious; and likewise, I mustn't know either. I'm in a constant interrogation: where does the deep and philosophical Dalí begin, and where does the loony and preposterous Dalí end?" Unfortunately, in the final years of his life, these two aspects of Dalí's personality (the inner fragmentation that Meryle Secrest detected in Dalí's *The Metamorphosis of Narcissus*) would blur until even Dalí was no longer able to quite distinguish between the two.

In one way, it is fair to say that from the mid–1950s on Dalí was very creative. Just as he had in the past branched out from painting into film, writing, jewelry, fashion, and set and costume design, he now turned his attention to television, holographs, and strange inventions, such as the Ovocipede, a vehicle consisting of a transparent plastic ball. Just as Dalí had shifted his theoretical focus from Freud to nuclear physics after World War II, he now became fascinated with the artistic implications of deoxyribonucleic acid (DNA), the molecular material that carries human genes. And just as he had begun a series of paintings on religious themes at the end of the 1940s, from the late 1950s through the 1960s he created a series of large "historical" canvases, such as *The Dream of Christopher Columbus.*

But what happened in the 1960s and 1970s was more than a shift in themes and interests. Dalí may have said that he liked Breton's anagram, but it is true that, at some point in the final decades of his life, he crossed a line and compromised his art for the sake of money. From "Bulletism," Dalí went on to design many items for sale: fabrics, shirts, cognac bottles, calendars, bathing suits, ashtrays for Air India, and gilded oyster knives. He associated himself with a perfume called "Rock and Roll" and painted a picture for the Vincent Price Art Collection at Sears, Roebuck. For $10,000, he endorsed Lanvin chocolates on French television. He appeared in another commercial for an airline, although he was known not to fly because of his fear of planes.

Still, everything Salvador did to earn money was not enough for Gala. As she grew older, her appetite for money and young lovers seemed to become insatiable. As Dalí himself aged, he was no longer able to put in 15-hour workdays as he had done earlier. Gala would lock him into a room, letting him out only

*Accompanied by members of his Court of Miracles, an aged Dalí leaves the Pompidou arts center in Paris in 1979 after he was barred by striking museum employees from an exhibition of his work. The strikers were protesting Dalí's support of the right-wing Franco regime in Spain.*

when he had finished a painting or design to fulfill a
contract. Ironically, Gala, who demanded more and
more money, handled the funds haphazardly. As cash,
checks, and bank notes poured into the Dalí household, she crammed them into suitcases, and much
potential income was lost because she forgot to cash
the checks or redeem the bank notes.

As Gala put increasing pressure on Dalí, and as
more and more middlemen were called in to handle
the ever-burgeoning number of contracts, some ques-
tionable maneuvers took place. On at least one occasion, Dalí signed blank sheets of paper that could then
be used for making "limited" editions of his lithographs. New printing technologies made it harder to
detect forgeries, and unscrupulous dealers took ad-
vantage of Dalí's carelessness. A great scandal erupted
when it turned out that the market was flooded with
"limited" editions of Dalí prints that were fakes. In
the 1980s, Dalí's New York attorney estimated that, by
charging up to $5,000 for cheap reproductions that
were worth about $5 each, counterfeiters had conser-
vatively sold one billion dollars' worth of fake Dalís in
the U.S. alone in just a few years' time.

As a public figure, Dalí was rediscovered by a new
generation in the 1960s. So-called hippies, who
wanted to live a nonconformist life, felt that Dalí
was a man they could model themselves after, and
Andy Warhol and other artists found inspiration in
Dalí's art. Dalí surrounded himself with a kind of
court, which included the talented and the bizarre,
the beautiful and the rich. Dalí called his entourage
the Court of Miracles, and he orchestrated the activities of his "court" into a kind of ongoing surrealistic
performance.

One night, as Dalí held forth at a New York bar
named Trader Vic's, Gala met the star of the rock
musical *Jesus Christ Superstar,* Jeff Fenholt. Gala, by

now even more removed from Dalí, became attached to Fenholt. This time, however, her interest was more than a passing one, and she and Fenholt spent weeks at a time in a castle that Dalí had purchased in Pubol, Spain. Eventually, Gala gave some of Dalí's artwork to Fenholt, who then auctioned off the pieces. This was the final blow for Dalí. He and Gala became so enraged at each other that they came to blows, resulting in injuries to both parties. Perhaps Dali was finally paying the price for failing to distinguish between not repressing the subconscious and giving himself over to it.

Dalí and Gala both suffered failing health at the end of the 1970s, and Gala died in 1982, completely estranged from her husband. Dalí's last years in the 1980s were sad: he suffered from Parkinson's disease and no longer had the mental or physical ability to paint as he once had. Occasionally, he would rally his forces and do some artwork. When he was in good health, he occupied himself with the museum that was being created in his honor in Figueres. Fortunately, he was surrounded by loving and loyal friends who visited him and attended to his every need. He also received several visits from the king of Spain, Juan Carlos I, who awarded Dalí the Grand Cross of Charles III and made him a marquis.

As Dalí's career was evaluated, other honors were bestowed on him. In 1980, London's Tate Gallery mounted a huge Dalí retrospective, which became the second most heavily attended exhibition in the museum's history. After viewing the show, art critic John McEwen wrote, "It is the spirit, the heroic scale and supreme attention to the detail of Dalí's pictorial defence—that is cowing. The fact that he has also found time to create a vast audience for painting . . . through his own remorseless exhibitionism . . . only increases one's sense of awe."

*Dalí's coffin is carried past the Teatro Museo Gala-Dalí on January 25, 1989. In addition to being a museum dedicated to his work, the unusual building served as Dalí's home during the final years of his life, when he was honored as Spain's foremost living artist.*

Finally, after suffering through a decade of severe illness, Dalí succumbed to heart failure on January 23, 1989. As he had requested, he was buried in his own museum in Figueres, the Teatro Museo Gala-Dalí, across from the church in which he had been baptized and three streets away from the house in which he had been born. After the funeral, Dalí's body was carried from the church by the museum's guards, who were dressed in uniforms that the artist had designed. Thousands of people stood in line for a last glimpse of the man who, since Picasso's death in 1973, had been the most famous living Spanish painter.

Today, Dalí and Picasso stand as the two greatest Spanish painters of the 20th century, and Dalí remains the preeminent figure in surrealism, a movement that profoundly influenced all the arts of the 20th century. Once, the young Catalan went to the Prado to study the canvases of the great masters; today, art students travel to the Teatro Museo Gala-Dalí, the most striking building in Figueres, to draw inspiration from the extraordinary works of Salvador Dalí. There is nothing more that an artist can desire.

# CHRONOLOGY

| | |
|---|---|
| 1904 | Born Salvador Dalí i Domènech in Figueres, Spain, on May 11 |
| 1919 | First public display of Dalí's paintings draws favorable critical attention |
| 1921 | Dalí enters Madrid's San Fernando Institute of Fine Arts |
| 1923 | Suspended from the San Fernando Institute after student protest |
| 1924 | Imprisoned for a month by the Primo de Rivera dictatorship; André Breton publishes his *Surrealist Manifesto,* beginning the surrealist movement |
| 1925 | Beginning of Dalí's romantic friendship with Federico García Lorca; Josép Dalmau organizes Dalí's first one-man show in Barcelona; Dalí reenrolls at the San Fernando Institute |
| 1926 | Meets Pablo Picasso during visit to Paris; expelled from the San Fernando Institute |
| 1927 | Paints his first surrealist-influenced work, *Honey Is Sweeter Than Blood* |
| 1928 | Criticizes the Catalonian avant-garde in his "Yellow Manifesto"; attacks Lorca's poetry, ending their relationship |
| 1929 | Collaborates with Luis Buñuel on *Un chien andalou;* paints *Dismal Sport;* becomes romantically involved with Gala Éluard |

| | |
|---|---|
| 1930 | Collaborates with Buñuel on film *L'age d'or*; settles with Gala in Port Lligat, Spain; *The Visible Woman* is published, expounding Dalí's "paranoiac-critical" method |
| 1931 | Dalí conceives of the "surrealist object" |
| 1934 | Marries Gala Éluard; makes first trip to the United States |
| 1936–39 | Spanish Civil War; Lorca is murdered by Fascists; Dalí switches support to Fascists after initially applauding the Communists and anarchists; Edward James becomes Dalí's associate and patron |
| 1937 | Dalí paints major paranoiac-critical work, *The Metamorphosis of Narcissus* |
| 1938 | Designs sets and costumes for ballet *Bacchanale* |
| 1939 | Breton expells Dalí from the surrealist movement |
| 1940 | The Dalís leave Europe to live in America |
| 1942 | Dalí's autobiography, *The Secret Life of Salvador Dalí,* is published |
| 1945 | Dalí collaborates with Alfred Hitchcock on *Spellbound*; develops interest in nuclear physics |
| 1948 | Returns to Spain, though he continues to visit Paris and New York |
| 1949 | Paints his first religious work, the *Madonna of Port Lligat* |
| 1952 | Tours the United States, speaking on his "mystical nuclear" art |
| 1955 | Lectures at the Sorbonne on the rhinoceros's horn and Vermeer's *Lacemaker* |

| | |
|---|---|
| 1956 | Illustrates *Don Quixote* through "Bulletism" |
| 1957 | *Dalí on Modern Art* is published |
| 1958 | Dalí exhibits atomic "anti-matter" paintings in New York |
| 1959 | Presents his Ovocipede, a vehicle consisting of a transparent plastic ball |
| 1963 | Publishes *The Tragic Myth of Millet's* The Angelus |
| 1964 | Is awarded one of Spain's highest decorations, the Grand Cross of Isabella the Catholic |
| 1966 | The New York Gallery of Modern Art presents Dalí's life works at the greatest retrospective show ever devoted to a living artist |
| 1967 | Rizzoli publishes an edition of the Bible illustrated by Dalí |
| 1968 | During May revolt in France, Dalí distributes tract, "My Cultural Revolution," to striking Sorbonne students |
| 1971 | Designs chess set for American Chess Foundation |
| 1972 | Devotes himself to engraving |
| 1978 | Elected to Beaux-Arts Academy |
| 1982 | Death of Gala Dalí; King Juan Carlos I of Spain awards Dalí the Grand Cross of Charles III and makes him a marquis; Dalí begins to suffer from Parkinsonism, which makes him an invalid for most of the decade |
| 1989 | Dies in Figueres on January 23 |

# FURTHER READING

Ades, Dawn. *Dalí.* New York: Thames and Hudson, 1990.

Alba, Victor. *Catalonia.* New York: Praeger, 1975.

Bosquet, Alain. *Conversations with Dalí.* New York: Dutton, 1969.

Buñuel, Luis. *My Last Sigh: The Autobiography of Luis Buñuel.* New York: Knopf, 1984.

Cheatham, Owen. *Dalí: Art-in-Jewels.* New York: Graphic Society, n.d.

Dalí, Ana Maria. *Salvador Dalí visto por su hermana.* Barcelona: Ediciones del Cotal, 1983.

Dalí, Salvador. *Dalí by Dalí.* New York: Abrams, 1970.

———. *Diary of a Genius.* New York: Doubleday, 1965.

———. *The Secret Life of Salvador Dalí.* New York: Dial Press, 1942.

———. *The Unspeakable Confessions of Salvador Dalí.* Translated by Harold J. Salemson. New York: Morrow, 1976.

Dalí, Salvador, with Philippe Halsman. *Dalí's Moustache: A Photographic Interview.* New York: Simon & Schuster, 1954.

Descharnes, Robert. *Salvador Dalí: The Work, the Man.* New York: Abrams, 1984.

Etherington-Smith, Meredith. *The Persistence of Memory.* New York: Random House, 1992.

Gibson, Ian. *Federico García Lorca: A Life.* New York: Pantheon, 1989.

Haslam, Malcolm. *The Real World of the Surrealists.* New York: Rizzoli, 1978.

Jean, Marcel, ed. *The Autobiography of Surrealism.* New York: Viking, 1980.

Longstreet, Stephen. *The Drawings of Dalí.* Los Angeles: Borden, 1964.

McGirk, Tim. *Wicked Lady: Salvador Dalí's Muse.* London: Hutchinson, 1989.

Morris, C. B. *Surrealism and Spain, 1920–1936.* Cambridge: Cambridge University Press, 1972.

Reed, Jan. *The Catalans.* London: Faber and Faber, 1978.

Rogerson, Mark. *The Dalí Scandal.* London: Gollancz, 1987.

Secrest, Meryle. *Salvador Dalí.* New York: Dutton, 1986.

Waldberg, Patrick. *Surrealism.* New York: Oxford University Press, 1978.

# INDEX

Ades, Dawn, 90

Alfonso XIII (king of Spain), 17, 25

*Andalusian Dog, An.* See *Un chien andalou*

"Aphrodisiac Jacket," 79

*Bacchanale,* 98

Ballets Russes de Monte Carlo, 98

Barcelona, Spain, 46, 50, 56, 58, 85

*Basket of Bread,* 50

Braque, Georges, 36

Breton, André, 54, 55, 58, 78, 80, 81, 88, 90, 102, 106

"Bulletism," 105, 106

Buñuel, Luis, 17, 38, 40, 41, 54, 56–57, 59, 64, 73

Cadaqués, Spain, 23–25, 42, 43, 46, 54, 62, 75, 77

Catalonia, Spain, 23, 42, 51, 79, 95

Chirico, Georgio de, 15, 61

*Christ of Saint John of the Cross,* 101

Crosby, Caresse, 95, 97

Cubism, 36, 37, 38

Dadaism, 38, 54, 55

Dalí, Ana María (sister), 21, 45, 64, 95, 100

Dalí, Felipa (mother), 21, 22, 23, 33

Dalí, Gala (wife), 62, 63–64, 74, 75, 77, 79, 83, 84, 85, 87, 88, 89, 92, 94, 95, 97, 106, 108
  death of, 109

Dalí, Salvador
  art training, 15–19, 30, 35–42
  autobiography, 95, 97, 98–99
  birth, 21
  childhood, 21–33
  death, 109–10
  education, 26–32
  exhibitions, 16, 32, 46, 47, 50, 63, 64, 83, 87–88, 90, 92–93, 97, 109
  films, 56–59, 63, 73, 75–76, 99
  lithographs and prints, 105, 108
  marriage, 83

paintings, 49–50, 51–52,
61, 62, 63, 77, 83, 89,
99–100, 101, 106
and surrealism, 51–55, 64,
78, 80–81, 83–84, 88,
89–90, 92, 103, 111
"Surrealist objects,"
78–79, 86
writings, 32, 46, 54, 55, 63,
77, 95
Dalí, Salvador, Sr. (father), 16,
19, 21, 22, 26, 28, 30, 32,
42, 44, 46, 49, 50, 57, 61,
64, 73, 75, 79, 100
Dalí, Tieta (stepmother),
42
Dalmau, Josép, 46, 47, 50
"Declaration of the
Independence of the
Imagination and of the
Rights of Man to His Own
Madness," 93
Dismal Sport, 61, 62, 63
Don Quixote (Cervantes), 105
Dream of Christopher Columbus,
The, 106
Dream of Venus, The, 93
Éluard, Paul, 55, 61, 83
Empardà, Spain, 23, 52,
75, 77
Ernst, Max, 55, 61, 76
Etherington-Smith, Meredith,
22, 61
Exploding Raphaelesque Head,
100
Figueres, Spain, 16, 21, 23, 30,
42, 46, 49, 109, 110

Forest of Gadgets, The, 51–52.
See also Honey Is Sweeter
Than Blood
France, 46, 47, 73, 94, 95, 103
Franco, Francisco, 86, 87
Freud, Sigmund, 36, 43, 52,
56, 90–92, 106
Futurism, 40, 55
Gaceta de los Artes magazine, 45
García Lorca, Federico, 17, 38,
43, 45, 46–47, 49–50, 51,
52, 54, 57 84, 85, 95
General and Technical Insti-
tute, 31, 32
Giraffes on Horseback Salad, 89
Goëmans, Camille, 58–59, 63,
64, 73, 74
Golden Age, The. See L'age d'or
Goya, Francisco de, 95
Grand Cross of Charles III,
109
Gris, Juan, 37
Hitchcock, Alfred, 99
Hitler, Adolf, 80, 81
Honey Is Sweeter Than Blood,
51–52, 61. See also The
Forest of Gadgets
Impressionism, 28, 30, 37
Internationalist Surrealist
Exhibition, 90
Interpretation of Dreams, The
(Freud), 43
James, Edward, 84, 85, 86, 87,
89, 92, 93, 94, 95, 97, 101
Juan Carlos I (king of Spain),
109
Klee, Paul, 55

*Labyrinth,* 98

*L'age d'or,* 73, 75–76

*L'Amic des Arts* magazine, 45

Leonardo da Vinci, 15

Levy, Julien, 83, 92, 93

Loeb, Pierre, 49

*Madonna of Port Lligat,* 99

Madrid, Spain, 17, 19, 32, 33, 38, 41, 45

Magritte, René, 55

Marx Brothers, 88–89

*Metamorphosis of Narcissus, The,* 89, 105

Michelangelo, 15

Miró, Joan, 37, 49, 55, 57, 76

Museum of Modern Art, 83, 87–88

Nazi party, 80, 81, 90, 95

Nogueres, Lidia, 25, 44, 52, 75, 89

Noi de Tona, 24

Núñez, Joan, 30, 35, 42

"Ode to Salvador Dalí" (García Lorca), 45

Ovocipede, 106

"Paranoiac-critical" method, 77–78, 89

Paris, France, 16, 19, 47, 49, 50, 54, 56, 57, 58, 61, 63, 64, 74, 75, 90, 97, 103

*Persistence of Memory, The,* 77, 83

*Persistence of Memory, The* (Etherington-Smith), 22

Picasso, Pablo, 15, 19, 36, 46, 63, 78, 83, 87, 103, 111

Pitxot, Lluís, 25, 26

Pitxot, Ramón, 16, 25, 27, 28

Pitxot, Ricardo, 25, 26

Pointillism, 28

Prado Museum, 38, 111

Raphael, 17, 100

Ray, Man, 55, 88

Residencia de Estudiantes, 17, 18, 35–36, 38, 43, 46

San Fernando Institute of Fine Arts, 15–18, 32, 35–42, 43, 46–47

Secrest, Meryle, 89, 105

*Secret Life of Salvador Dalí, The,* 95, 97, 98–99

Spain, 21, 22, 35, 47, 54, 61, 79, 87, 100, 103

Spanish Civil War, 86–87, 91

*Spellbound,* 99

*Still Life by Moonlight,* 49–50

Surrealism, 51–55, 56, 62, 64, 76, 78, 80–81, 83–84, 88, 89–90, 92, 103, 111

Tanguy, Yves, 55, 76

Teatro Museo Gala-Dalí, 110, 111

Thirion, André, 78

*Un chien andalou* 56–58, 59, 63, 73

United States, 83, 95, 102

Van Gogh, Vincent, 30

Vermeer, Jan, 103

*Visible Woman, The,* 77

Warhol, Andy, 108

World's Fair of 1939, 93–94

World War I, 38

World War II, 87, 99, 100, 102, 106

**DAVID CARTER** studied French literature at Emory University and the Sorbonne. After receiving his M.A. at the University of Wisconsin-Madison, he made a documentary film with Peter Townshend on the Indian spiritual master Meher Baba. An editor who lives in New York City, Carter is also the author of *George Santayana* in Chelsea House's HISPANICS OF ACHIEVEMENT series.

**RODOLFO CARDONA** is professor of Spanish and comparative literature at Boston University. A renowned scholar, he has written many works of criticism, including *Ramón, a Study of Gómez de la Serna and His Works* and *Visión del esperpento: Teoría y práctica del esperpento en Valle-Inclán*. Born in San José, Costa Rica, he earned his B.A. and M.A. from Louisiana State University and received a Ph.D. from the University of Washington. He has taught at Case Western Reserve University, the University of Pittsburgh, the University of Texas at Austin, the University of New Mexico, and Harvard University.

**JAMES COCKCROFT** is currently a visiting professor of Latin American and Caribbean studies at the State University of New York at Albany. A three-time Fulbright scholar, he earned a Ph.D. from Stanford University and has taught at the University of Massachusetts, the University of Vermont, and the University of Connecticut. He is the author or coauthor of numerous books on Latin American subjects, including *Neighbors in Turmoil: Latin America, The Hispanic Experience in the United States: Contemporary Issues and Perspectives,* and *Outlaws in the Promised Land: Mexican Immigrant Workers and America's Future.*